GREENHOUSE GARDENING

A Step-By-Step Guide on How to Grow Foods and Plants for Beginners

By Joseph Bosner

GREENHOUSE GARDENING

© Copyright 2019 - All rights reserved.

The content contained within this book may not be reproduced, duplicated or transmitted without direct written permission from the author or the publisher.

Under no circumstances will any blame or legal responsibility be held against the publisher, or author, for any damages, reparation, or monetary loss due to the information contained within this book. Either directly or indirectly.

Legal Notice:

This book is copyright protected. This book is only for personal use. You cannot amend, distribute, sell, use, quote or paraphrase any part, or the content within this book, without the consent of the author or publisher.

Disclaimer Notice:

Please note the information contained within this document is for educational and entertainment purposes only. All effort has been executed to present accurate, up to date, and reliable, complete information. No warranties of any kind are declared or implied. Readers acknowledge that the author is not engaging in the rendering of legal, financial, medical or professional advice. The content within this book has been derived from various sources.

GREENHOUSE GARDENING

Please consult a licensed professional before attempting any techniques outlined in this book.

By reading this document, the reader agrees that under no circumstances is the author responsible for any losses, direct or indirect, which are incurred as a result of the use of information contained within this document, including, but not limited to, — errors, omissions, or inaccuracies.

Table of contents

INTRODUCTION .... **XI**

CHAPTER 1 BENEFITS OF A GREENHOUSE 1

GARDEN OF EDEN.. 1
VARIETY IS SPICE! 3
PROTECTION DETAIL.. 4
DON'T BUG ME!... 5
ENERGY EFFICIENT 6
PLANTING SOME ZEN IN YOUR LIFE.. 7

CHAPTER 2 CHOOSING A GREENHOUSE 10

STEP 1: LOCATION 10
  Oh Greenhouse, Where Art Thou? - The Ideal Location............. 10
  Truly Electrifying... 11
  Drain the System... 11
STEP 2: DESIGNING AND BUILDING A GREENHOUSE........... 12
  Lean-to... 13
  Quonset Frame.. 14
  Free Standing.. 15
  Other Options.. 15
STEP 3: FRAME AND GLORY - CHOOSING A FRAME
MATERIAL.. 16
  Wood.. 17
  Steel... 17

GREENHOUSE GARDENING

Aluminum 18

Plastic 18

STEP 4: UNDERCOVER OPERATIONS - CHOOSING THE
COVER MATERIALS 18

Plastic 19

Polycarbonate 19

Acrylic 20

Fiberglass 20

Glass 21

YOU'RE GROUNDED! 22

GARDEN BEDSIDE MANNERS 22

Clay 27

Silt 27

Loam 27

Chalky 28

Sandy 29

Peat 29

BUYING A USED GREENHOUSE 30

Size 30

Space 32

Frame 33

Cover 34

PROFESSIONAL GREENHOUSE 35

COMMERCIAL GREENHOUSES 36

HOBBY GREENHOUSES 37

CHAPTER 3 GREENHOUSE ENVIRONMENT 39

GREENHOUSE GARDENING

Seasons Greetings - Working With Greenhouse Seasons.. 40
    Microclimates *42*
Grouping 42
Mulch 42
Wind blocks 43
Water 43
It Is That Time Of The Season 43
    Warm Season Crops *45*
For Winter 45
Temperature 47
Airflow 48
Water 49
For Summer 49
Humidity 50
Water 51
Ventilation 52
Shading 52
Dampness 53
For Spring 54
For Autumn/Fall 55

CHAPTER 4 PROTECTING YOUR GREENHOUSE . 56

Gone With The Wind - Wind Protection 56
Pest Control - Managing Pests 59
    Join the Resistance! *61*
    Inviting Less Pests *62*

GREENHOUSE GARDENING

- *Go Easy on the Fertilizer* *65*
- *Clean Up Other Materials* *66*
- *Make Friends With Creatures* *66*
- *Identifying Dangers* *66*
- *Knowing How To Deal With Your Pest* *68*
- *Choose Your Control Method* *69*
- *Physical Control Methods* *69*
- *Biological Control Methods* *71*
- *Other Control Methods* *72*

CENTER FOR DISEASE CONTROL - PROTECTING AGAINST DISEASES 75

- *Maintain Soil Health* *75*
- *Remove Mildew* *76*
- *Drip Irrigation* *77*

PROTECTION DETAIL - KEEPING YOURSELF PROTECTED . 78

CHAPTER 5 ESSENTIAL GREENHOUSE EQUIPMENT 80

- DIGGING TOOLS 81
  - *Shovel/Spade* *81*
  - *Trowel* *82*
  - *Forks* *83*
- CULTIVATING TOOLS 83
  - *Hoes* *84*
  - *Weeder* *84*
- CUTTING TOOLS 85
  - *Pruners* *85*

Hedge Shears *86*
Lopper *87*
Pruning Saw *87*

CHAPTER 6 PLANT PROPAGATION 88

WHAT IS PLANT PROPAGATION? 88

SEED PROPAGATION 90

CLONING 91

CHAPTER 7 HOW TO GROW WITHOUT SOIL 95

CHAPTER 8 GROUND VERSUS CONTAINER 100

CHAPTER 9 POLLINATION 104

POLLINATING MANUALLY 105

POLLINATING BY USING DEVICES 106

POLLINATION BY BEES 106

CHAPTER 10 GROWING FRUITS, HERBS AND VEGETABLES 108

FRUITS 110

Size *112*
Pollination *113*
Buy Plants, Not Seeds *114*
Buy high-quality plants *114*
Certified and Tested *114*
Inspect *115*
Planting the Fruit *115*

HERBS 120

Planting Herbs *121*

Timing *121*

Planting Your Herbs *123*

Caring for Your Herb *124*

VEGETABLES 125

Location *125*

More Sunlight *126*

Planting Methods *126*

Natural Ground *126*

Raised Beds *127*

Soil Tactics *127*

Using Seeds *128*

Sowing Your Vegetables *129*

Fertilizing Your Vegetable Garden *130*

CHAPTER 11 GROWING FLOWERS AND PLANTS . 132

Discover Flowers *132*

Warm Season Annuals *133*

Cool Season Annuals *133*

FLOWER GARDEN TIPS 134

Choosing Your Color Palette *134*

Working with the Shape of Your Flowers *137*

Working with Layers *138*

PLANTING YOUR FLOWERS 138

CHAPTER 12 GREENHOUSE BUSINESS 140

CHOOSE WHAT YOU WANT TO SELL 141

IT IS NOT ALL ABOUT NUMBERS 141

GREENHOUSE GARDENING

- Selling Your Plants 142
  - *Farmer's Market* 142
  - *Online Listings* 142
  - *Yard Sales* 143
- Marketing Your Garden 143
  - *Create Flyers* 143
  - *Word-of-Mouth* 144
  - *Create a Classifieds Ad* 144
  - *Open a Social Media Page* 145

CONCLUSION **147**

INTRODUCTION

It was circa 30 A.D., and the emperor Tiberius needed more cucumbers.

More specifically, he needed one cucumber a day, according to his physicians, to help him with an ailment. Which is why Roman engineers and gardeners had to find a way to maintain a continuous production of cucumbers, which would not have been a challenge if not for the fact that they had to provide these cucumbers specifically for the emperor all year round.

So they decided to brainstorm: How does one grow the same plant throughout the year?

You see, cucumbers flourish during warm and moist seasons. This means the physicians had to find a way to raise cucumbers during the snowy winters. Yes, it did snow in the Roman Empire. Not everything in Rome was about politics and gladiator fights on a hot and sunny day.

To solve the problem for the emperor, the engineers used a wheeled cart to carry the cucumbers and placed the cart under the sun. This gave the cucumbers the necessary warmth they needed. When night arrived (or when it was winter), a special cover made from frames coated with transparent materials housed the cucumbers, keeping them warm.

By doing this, the engineers helped the emperor dig his teeth into some delicious gourds. After all, a cucumber a day keeps the physicians away (or those backstabbing politicians away; it was Rome after all).

But the point I am trying to make here is that greenhouses are not a recent invention. They have been part of human history for centuries. This fact is not so surprising. After all, agriculture developed thousands of years before humans began to write. It would not be a stretch to imagine that someone figured out how to produce crops at any time during the year.

Greenhouses are mostly transparent structures where plants are grown. You can typically find them in cold regions like parts of Canada, Finland, and Greenland, but they are not confined to those countries. The transparent covering is usually made of glass and allows sunlight to pass through during the day. During nighttime, the glass traps the heat inside, continuing to keep the plants warm despite the temperatures outside.

It is an ingenious invention that makes use of physics. Today, you can find the name associated with climate change.

Greenhouses themselves are not responsible for climate change, but the name is used to describe the process that causes temperatures to increase on the Earth's surface; the greenhouse effect. In this effect, gases such as carbon dioxide trap the heat from the sun, just like the glass roofs of greenhouses.

People who are unaware of the functions of greenhouses often wonder if the structures cause harm to the environment. But research has shown that these glassed structures are indeed environmentally friendly, and not just that. They are sustainable, as well. Greenhouses have also been known to contribute towards a better climate. Not directly, of course. But they do have an indirect effect.

Many countries that require plants and crops often have to import them. This means that they have to rely on ships and planes that burn fuel to reach their destinations, exhausting carbon dioxide into the air on their journey. By using greenhouses, the countries can be self-reliant and maintain a sustainable form of food production for years. That minimizes the usage of ships and planes, which in turn reduces the amount of carbon dioxide spewed into the air. The result is a minor improvement in the global climate, but an improvement nonetheless.

Throughout this book, you will learn about these incredible structures and how you can maintain one on your own.

You will learn why they are useful (apart from keeping

ships and planes from dispersing carbon dioxide), how they can help you create some delicious food filled with natural and home-grown ingredients, and how you can even use them to raise beautiful plants and flowers.

So if you are ready, let us add a slice of nature in your backyard!

CHAPTER 1

BENEFITS OF A GREENHOUSE

Garden of Eden

There are plants that grow well during the summer, utilizing the abundant sunlight available. Then there are those plants that grow well during the winter, finding the cold weather more comfortable. Greenhouses help maintain a stable temperature within its facility, whether it is in the middle of the summer or during freezing winters.

Plants that are subjected to abrupt changes in temperatures do not grow healthily. They are at a risk of losing their nutrients and even growing stunted.

GREENHOUSE GARDENING

With greenhouses, you are providing a controlled environment for plants and herbs to not merely grow, but thrive. In fact, you can even add specific features to your greenhouse - such as ventilation systems - to keep conditions just the way you, or your plants, like them. This becomes essential for growing certain types of crops, herbs, flowers, or plants.

For example, you can start raising fruits like tomatoes. Yes, they are fruits. Science has helped settle the age-long debate about whether tomatoes belong in the fruit category or not.

By the way, if you ever want to prove to anyone that they are fruits, here is how: tomatoes grow in the ovaries present at the base of the flower and include the seeds of the plant inside them. These are typical characteristics of true fruits. Using this distinct feature, scientists placed the popular red berry in the fruit category. So yes, they are berries, too.

But I digress. Let us get back to raising tomatoes within a greenhouse and how they can survive any weather. You see, by growing tomatoes in a greenhouse during the summer, you allow them to mature. When these fruits mature, they have the right fortitude to survive the winter. This in turn helps them stay healthy during cold weather. The result? Delicious, sweet, and fresh tomatoes for your cooking.

Even during heavy rainfall, you do not have to worry

about your plants or crops drowning (more on how they can drown further into the book, when we discuss how to maintain crops). The enclosed conditions of the greenhouse ensure that you can keep everything dry within it, making it perfect for when you want to garden or grow something during the rainy season.

Variety is Spice!

With the right conditions, there are a number of plants that you can grow in a greenhouse. Do you need some vegetables? Get your greenhouse ready for vegetables (and fruits) such as tomatoes, peppers, and even cucumbers (whether you are an emperor/empress who needs them daily or not). Are you interested in raising crops? Because you can work with options such as broccoli, lettuce, peas, and carrots.

From warm-seasoned crops to cold-season crops; from ornamentals to even tropical flowers, you can grow a plethora of plants right in your backyard!

You can use what you produce in your greenhouse to decorate your house or create your own garden. When you perfect your techniques, you can even sell your products at the local market. And if you do not want to grow your plants to sell them, that's okay, too.

Maintaining a greenhouse is a joy-filled hobby (but

more on that later). When it comes to cooking, you can focus on those ingredients that you use frequently. By growing these ingredients in your backyard, you save a lot on your trip to the local store.

Protection Detail

In 2018, an army of worms, rats, and birds decimated nearly 17,000 hectares of crops in the east-African country of Tanzania. The damage was so severe that officials feared food shortage in various areas of the district.

You might think that such incidences are restricted to a certain country or region. However, around the world, pests are known to eradicate the produce of farmers and cause food problems.

When you are raising crops and plants, pests become a common enemy. From ants, to flies, wasps, aphids, and beetles, crops and plants might come under attack numerous times during the year. Each country in the world is home to numerous pests. However, some creatures are found abundantly in one region or country and less (and sometimes never) in another location.

For example, tobacco whiteflies are common pests in regions such as Asia, Africa, and Europe, but are not typically found in North America. However, fall armyworms are found in regions such as North and South American, Africa, and certain parts of Europe.

Regardless of where you are and what pest plagues your region, the crops and plants in your region face a threat from these creatures.

Using greenhouses, you are giving plants a safe place to grow and in turn, they reward you in many ways. While it is true that pests are capable of attacking greenhouses as well, you have a better chance of getting rid of them.

Don't Bug Me!

You do not need pests to ruin plants. Even insects that are commonly found in practically every region on the planet can also cause a lot of harm.

Whether they are ants or houseflies, they are capable of causing much destruction to plants and crops. One of the ways that they can do this is by directly attacking the plants.

Another method is by causing harm indirectly. Insects can do this by spreading infections or diseases to the crops. These diseases can be viral, bacterial, or even fungal. By simply affecting a few crops, insects can ensure that the diseases spread to nearby plants, which in turn carry the infection further.

Wherever these insects cause damage, they often multiply and grow in the same area. This prevents farmers and gardeners from growing crops in that location again. Eventually, the insects and their offspring have to be dealt with (which is a painstakingly lengthy process) before growing any produce.

Greenhouses provide you a solution to the insect problem in the form of raised beds. You will learn more about these structures later, but essentially, they are containers that hold plants. In the event of an insect infestation, you can easily clean out the raised beds and plant crops again.

Energy Efficient

Greenhouses use sunlight, for the most part. This creates a natural lighting and heating system for the plants, which is in turn essential for the process known as photosynthesis. In this process, the plants convert carbon dioxide into essential nutrients using the light from the sun.

Furthermore, light is also involved in a process called transpiration. Think of this process as the way in which plants breathe, and it usually occurs during the early hours of the day. In this process, light enters tiny pores that are present on the surface of leaves and allows the plant to receive gases from the environment.

All of this is essential to keep your plants and crops healthy.

What makes using greenhouses beneficial is that by using natural light, you are reducing the reliance on electrically supplied lighting. When this happens, you are removing high consumption of energy from the equation. People have this notion that greenhouse tap into a lot of electricity for maintenance. This is not true, unless you personally choose to add certain features to the greenhouse that require power. While greenhouses do consume electricity, you can design yours in such a way that it minimizes electricity usage.

With greenhouses, you are mainly depending on what nature is already providing you in abundance.

Planting Some Zen in Your Life

You read that right. Greenhouses help you relieve stress and bring a sense of calm into your life. This might sound like a metaphysical or spiritual approach to looking at greenhouses. However, science has some answers for why you feel relaxed inside greenhouses.

According to the National Center for Biotechnology

Information[1], engaging with indoor plants has led to the reduction of not just psychological, but physiological stress. By conducting a simple experiment involving young adults, they noticed that participants of the experiment began to show feelings of comfort and calm after working with indoor plants.

What you experience in your environment through sight, sounds, and even touch affects your mood in many ways. In fact, studies have shown that by just looking at scenes of nature, you are reducing negative feelings within you.

In a greenhouse, you are not just looking at nature in your own backyard, but you are actually part of it. This has an even greater effect on your well-being and your health.

First, your stress lowers. This means that you are able to focus better on your life and other tasks. Nature has been known to calm anger, which in turn helps you control your emotions better. Being in nature has also been known to help people deal with negative states of mind, from fear to depression to sadness, by creating positive impressions on people's emotions and mental state.

---

[1] MM, T. (2019). Therapeutic effects of an indoor gardening programme for older people living in nursing homes. - PubMed - NCBI. Retrieved from
https://www.ncbi.nlm.nih.gov/pubmed/20492039

GREENHOUSE GARDENING

CHAPTER 2

CHOOSING A GREENHOUSE

Step 1: Location

Before you decide to erect a greenhouse in your backyard, you should note down a few essential points.

Oh Greenhouse, Where Art Thou? - The Ideal Location

The location of your greenhouse becomes an important factor, because you need to decide how far away from or close to your home you would like your greenhouse to be. Ideally, you should pick a location that provides sufficient sunlight. This means that you should keep it as far as possible from the cover of trees or nearby structures.

GREENHOUSE GARDENING

This is particularly important during the winter, because the winter sun has a low angle, which causes even short trees and buildings to block it entirely. When this happens, plants receive less sunlight than is necessary for their growth.

Truly Electrifying

Choose a location that provides you with access to electricity. One of the reasons you might need electricity is to help you manage your greenhouse more. You won't be necessarily using a lot of power (or you actually may not need it at all), but it is handy to have access to electricity. You might require additional cables to bring power to the greenhouse, but ensure you are not building the greenhouse too far from the nearest electrical supply, or you might have to invest in long cables.

If the greenhouse is attached to your home, then it becomes easier for you to run cables into the structure. However, if the greenhouse is located outside, there is the chance that you might need the help of an electrician to help you find the most efficient way to run power to your greenhouse.

Drain the System

You need an area that allows you to construct an efficient drainage system. This is useful for syphoning away excess water. If you are unsure of what criteria satisfies a location that can provide proper drainage, then you should ideally look for level ground. If the location you chose is uneven, then you might have to fill the area to encourage a proper drainage system. Uneven ground can collect water, often attracting insects and certain plant infections.

Step 2: Designing and Building a Greenhouse

When you have confirmed the location for your greenhouse, then your next step is to design and build it. Before you bring out your hammer and nails, let us consider an important factor; you need to decide what you greenhouse's dimensions are going to be. Would you like it to be the size of a small shack, or are you planning on creating the greenhouse from Jurassic Park, minus the T-Rex?

Choosing the size of your greenhouse plays an important role in its maintenance. When you have a small greenhouse, your costs are low and you do not require a lot of heat to keep it warm. On the other hand, larger greenhouses give you more space, allowing you to plant a variety of crops.

If you find yourself lost when picking the size of the greenhouse, then consider the type of plants and crops you would like to grow. If you have a lot of plants in your inventory, then perhaps you might need a large space to grow all of them. If you have fewer plants, then you might not require a big greenhouse.

The minimum size that you should ideally consider for a greenhouse is 10 feet by 10 feet. However, you can also consider 8 feet by 6 feet. These size options might provide you with a smaller space, but they have the benefit of being inexpensive. Furthermore, if you are a beginner, then you might want to try using a smaller structure in the beginning. Maintaining plants within a small space is easier and lets you practice your gardening skills properly.

When you have chosen the size of the greenhouse, there are a few options for structure.

Lean-to

If you are planning to locate your greenhouse against your house or a building, then you can create a structure that leans on the wall of the property.

This allows you to use the wall of the building to cover one side of the greenhouse. Additionally, if the wall is made of bricks, then it will generate enough heat to keep the greenhouse warm as well. You can then use wooden beams or rebar to create support mechanisms for the greenhouse.

GREENHOUSE GARDENING

Quonset Frame

You could also think of building a Quonset frame. These frames are basically domed ceilings on top of the greenhouse that are built using materials such steel or PVC. While quonset frames are not a mandatory inclusion, they have their benefits. For one, they are proven to retain more heat from the sun. I personally recommend avoiding PVC, as it may release estrogenic chemicals that are soluble in water. You should go ahead with low-density polyethylene, a much safer form of plastic.

Figure 1: A simple greenhouse with a quonset frame, or a domed roof.

Remember that you can use inexpensive materials to build the frame as well. However, bear in mind that the cheaper the materials, the less durable the frame might be. More on frame materials further in the next section of this chapter.

Free Standing

You might be able to guess what I am talking about by reading the title alone. Essentially, free standing greenhouses do not require the support of any other buildings nearby. They are standalone structures that usually stand apart from your home or building.

Free standing greenhouses are used when you have a specific design in mind or when there is not enough sunlight near your home for a lean-to structure.

Other Options

You do not have to limit yourself to a few options. In fact, you could add the frames by yourself depending on the type of greenhouse you want to build, or you could get the assistance of a builder to do the job for you. Unless you are a designer yourself, I recommend that you get help. There are a few reasons for this:

- You get to save time on your project. The builder will know how to build your greenhouse as fast as possible.

- You get incredible input. After all, you might be certain of your plans, but what if there was a better way to do it? What if all you required was a simple extension that could save you a lot of money? By using a professional, you get to acquire valuable insights into your greenhouse's design, location, and other factors, and sometimes even learn how you can effectively maintain it in the long run.

- This might sound rather farfetched, but you could even save money in certain circumstances. When you set out to build a greenhouse, you could end up creating a structure that might not meet your plans. When that happens, you might have to dismantle what you have built so far. That means you might have to purchase new materials. With a professional designer, your work gets completed smoothly and with minimal mistakes.

Step 3: Frame and Glory - Choosing a Frame Material

You can work with many materials for the design of your greenhouse. Each material provides its own set of advantages. When choosing materials, think about how much you are willing to spend on them, if they are ideal for the weather conditions in your region, and how much time you are willing to invest in their maintenance. Here are a few options:

GREENHOUSE GARDENING

Wood

For DIYers (do-it-yourselfers), wood is the material of choice. It is readily available in the market and people often build up a workshop in their garage or backyard in order to use wood. It is an easy material to work with as well. The drawback to wood is that unlike other materials, it can rot over time. This means that you might need to maintain it properly and provide proper drainage in your greenhouse to prevent the material from getting damp easily. However, wood is a versatile material. What I mean is that you can install attachments (such as hooks) on it, run cables through it, and more. You can even add a lot more holding and storage options to your greenhouse if it is made of wood. All you need is a storage structure and some nails.

Steel

Steel is one of the toughest frames in the market. You will often spot steel frames used on large greenhouses that serve a commercial purpose. Steel is one of the most expensive materials to use for your greenhouse, but it adds more durability to the structure. Steel also anchors your greenhouse much more securely than other materials, which might be a useful feature to consider if you live in an area with strong winds. Ideally, you should look for the other frame material options on this list.

Aluminum

These frames are durable and lightweight. They add strength to your greenhouse and are cheaper to use than steel. However, because of their lightweight design, you can find them connected to steel foundations at the bottom to hold them in place properly. One of the best aspects of aluminum is that it is a good conductor of heat. During daytime and in summer, they can retain heat well. This heat retention helps your plants grow better and even supplies them heat during the night.

Plastic

Plastic is a flexible and lightweight material that is ideal for the budget-friendly gardener. It is a good material to use when constructing small greenhouses. It does not retain heat as well as steel or aluminum, as plastic is a poor conductor of heat, but it is easy to work with and also offers a small degree of durability.

Step 4: Undercover Operations - Choosing the Cover Materials

Once you have decided how you would like to approach the frame of your greenhouse, it is time to work on the cover.

GREENHOUSE GARDENING

Plastic

While most people might think of using glass for their greenhouse, it is important to know that glass might require a bit more investment from your side. The other alternative to glass is using plastic, which does not trap heat as much as glass but is ideal for getting started with your greenhouse. Plastic also provides a good cover for lean-to structures (those that lean against a wall), Quonset framed greenhouses, and other small framed greenhouses.

Plastic comes in various forms. When you are working with your greenhouse, make sure you choose your plastic carefully. For example, PET is an inexpensive material that is also readily available. It is easy to use and is typically affordable. However, it is known to have a short life, so you might have to replace it frequently. You could instead choose to use LDPE, or low-density polyethylene. LDPE is another form of plastic that is a bit more pricey, but one that lasts longer.

Polycarbonate

You can choose to use polycarbonate panels for your greenhouse. The best part about this material is that it is slightly flexible, giving you more ways to work with your greenhouse. Additionally, polycarbonate is stronger that regular plastic and does not crack like glass. However, the material is mostly translucent. This means that it does not let in sunlight as much as glass does. Do note that polycarbonate could contain certain industrial chemicals, so you should always choose to pick one that is of high quality.

Acrylic

Also know as Plexiglas, you can use acrylic if you would prefer to have more transparency than polycarbonate. Acrylic also provides a degree of flexibility, allowing you to work with most types of greenhouses. It is fairly strong and durable, giving your greenhouse a fair amount of protection. Do note that acrylic is weaker than polycarbonate, so you cannot rely on it when it comes to physical damage.

Fiberglass

One of the inexpensive, and sturdy, options as far as plastics go would be fiberglass. While you might not often spot translucent fiberglass on the market, you can easily get transparent fiberglass sheets to help you get the job done on your greenhouse. The only drawback to this material is the fact that it does not stay clear for a long period. The plastic loses its transparency faster than both polycarbonate and acrylic.

GREENHOUSE GARDENING

Glass

Finally, you can choose glass as the covering material. If you have seen any pictures or videos of a greenhouse, then you might be aware that they are usually shown with glass paneling. Glass is definitely the most aesthetically appealing material for greenhouses. Glass also provides the most transparency, which in turn filters in the most sunlight. Here are a few points to remember when opting for glass coverings:

- Glass is an expensive material. Depending on the size of your greenhouse, you might have to spend more to get the right number of sheets.

- Expounding on the above point; remember that a tiny crack might become a costly replacement.

- Consider looking at different builders and suppliers to purchase glass. This is to ensure that you get the best price and find the right number of glass panes for your greenhouse. If you are planning to install the glass yourself, then researching the right amount of glass required for the greenhouse helps save money, as you won't spend unnecessarily on a large order of glass.

You're Grounded!

If you like, you can create ground conditions that are ideal for your greenhouse. Although this step is not entirely necessary, it will help add a better drainage system for your greenhouse.

You can choose to pour gravel on the ground as a foundation. This will allow additional drainage for the greenhouse and adds a nice leveled surface for you to walk on. A tip for you to follow is to first measure the area that your greenhouse occupies. Using wooden stakes (or just about any material), mark the border of your greenhouse. This will give you an idea of the space available for you to add gravel or concrete. Using measurements creates a clean working space.

Garden Bedside Manners

To grow any plant, you need to ensure that it has the right soil for cultivation.

You can use the soil already available to you in the garden, or you could add raised beds in your greenhouse. If you are using gravel on the ground, or if you are planning to build your greenhouse on a hard surface like concrete or hard-packed soil, then raised beds would be a good option to grow your plants. A raised bed is a type of container that houses your plants. Typically, they are square or rectangular in shape and come in various lengths, depending on the garden, the type of crops, or other factors. One of the reasons why raised beds are preferred by many gardeners is because you can add soil into them, especially when there is no proper soil to work with (or when the ground is hard). You can even get yourself different kinds of raised beds to have the soil depth necessary for growing your plants.

Here is an example of a raised bed:

Figure 2: A raised bed

As you can see from the image above, the gardener has placed a tall raised bed in his or her backyard. The idea behind the arrangement is to grow plants within a small container-like space that also allows you to fill it up with soil.

In the image above, the raised bed is slightly tall. This is an intentional design to hold plants with deep roots. If your raised bed is too shallow, then the roots of certain plants might end up hitting the bottom. This inhibits the healthy growth of the plants. On the other hand, crops with short roots might require short raised beds. Always know what plants or crops you would like to grow before deciding on the type of raised bed you want to use.

When you are choosing a raised bed, you might want to keep the following pointers in mind.

- Some surfaces are covered in grass. It is better to remove the grass before using the surface for your raised beds. However, if you have ever worked on grass before, then you might be aware just how cumbersome it can get to remove it. My recommendation to you is; don't even try removing it. Simply cover the grass with any inexpensive material like cardboard (**Pro tip:** some supermarkets and local stores do not mind giving away used cardboard boxes, so go ahead and get them. Yay to free stuff!). After placing the covering material, place a layer of soil over it (nothing too much, just enough to hide the material). You can now place your flower bed on a grass-free surface. If you would like to remove the grass entirely, then wait for the grass to break down (which it will over time since the material placed above deprives it of sunlight).

- Quite often, gardeners find it convenient to connect a rudimentary form of an irrigation system to their raised beds. The way they do this is by connecting one end of a hose to a water tap and lead the other to the raised bed. If you would like to create a similar setup, make sure you do it before filling your raised bed with soil. This will allow you to plan the placement of your raised bed effectively.

- When you are starting out, you might find it difficult to know just how much soil your raised bed might require. There are plenty of soil calculators online that can help you get the ideal amount to fill your raised bed. Gardener's.com and SoilCalculator.com are some online portals that you can use to measure soil quantity. Do note that whatever measurements you discover after using the calculator, it is always preferable to get good quality soil and fertilizer in the market. This helps you grow better plants.

If you prefer to use a garden bed instead, then you

might need to assess an area before digging up your garden.

Figure 3: Using natural ground, or the garden bed, to plant crops

One of the vital components of your assessment is whether your potential garden bed has any gas lines underneath. You do not want to get in trouble with the gas company just because you wanted to grow some carrots!

Next, you need to check the type of soil. Is it a peaty, loamy, or a clay soil? Each variation has its own advantages.

Let us look at a few types of soils you might be working with.

Clay

Clay soil is rich in nutrients, but that is its only redeeming quality. These kinds of soils get unshapely and sticky when they are damp and are fairly solid when they are dry. They do not leave a lot of room for drainage. However, if you can create an efficient drainage system, then you can make use of the nutrients that they provide. If you do not have any other soil nearby and you want to use a clay soil, then make sure you fertilize it properly and add a drainage system.

Silt

One of the best features of this soil is its ability to retain moisture. This helps in providing sufficient water to the roots of plants. Additionally, the soil also packs many nutrients, making it ideal for numerous plants. You can cultivate the soil easily, but to do that, you might have to provide and maintain a proper drainage system.

Loam

A loamy soil is composed of silt, sand, and small traces of clay. The soil can hold moisture and contains enough nutrients for plant growth (because of the combination of various soil types). However, it does not release all that moisture easily, even during summer. When there is sunlight, loamy soil can heat up rather quickly. You might require a good ventilation system in your greenhouse to work with loamy soil. You might also require a lot more fertilizer than other forms of soil to work with loam.

Chalky

These soils are always alkaline. To understand what that means, let us step into the world of chemistry (trust me, this is going to be fun.) To measure the alkalinity of soil, a special scale called the pH scale is used. This scale features numbers from zero to fourteen, with the number seven denoting neutrality. If the measurement of a substance falls below seven, then the substance is acidic, and if it falls above seven, then it is alkaline. When a soil falls into the alkaline category (meaning, it has a pH level over seven), then it tends to contain substances like magnesium and sodium. These substances tend to affect the growth of a plant. Sodium, for example, can cause surplus toxicity in plants. It drains out water from plant tissues, causing them to dry out. As you can see, this is not what we need for the plants that we are planning to grow in our greenhouses.

On the other hand, chalky soil tends to hold many essential nutrients for plants. If you find yourself having to deal with chalky soil and do not have other options, then worry not. All you have to do is utilize high-quality fertilizers, especially those that can balance the pH levels of the soil. You can also get yourself humus, a special type of organic matter that helps retain water better.

Sandy

The texture of a sandy soil feels granular. The main advantage of this soil is that it can heat up pretty fast (anyone who has been to the beach during summer know how hot sand can get). The soil drains moisture excessively and dehydrates quickly during summer. Sandy soil is a difficult soil to work with, as it offers poor conditions for plant growth. Should you find yourself dealing with this type of soil, then using organic fertilizer might benefit you greatly. Ideally, I would recommend kelp meal fertilizers for the job. Additionally, having a proper irrigation system to supply sufficient water does wonders when working with sandy soil.

Peat

Peaty soil prevents the soil from holding too many nutrients. Why? Because it is acidic for peat's sake (pun intended)! Puns aside, working with peaty soil means you need proper drainage. This is because the soil retains water, especially during spring and when there is heavy rainfall. You can find many nutrients in peaty soil, making it beneficial for healthy plant growth.

Ensure that you reduce the acidity of the soil by either using the right fertilizer or substances like glacial rock dust that help in raising the pH levels of the soil.

Now that you know about the various soil types, you are better prepared to work on your greenhouse. If you find yourself confused about fertilizers, always get assistance from the local garden supply store. They will be able to help you find the right organic matter for your soil and provide you with helpful tips.

Buying a Used Greenhouse

When you feel that you just want to get down to the good stuff, then you might prefer to buy a greenhouse instead. If you are seeking to purchase a greenhouse, there are a few factors that you should consider (trust me, it is not as easy as "I think that price is right so that is probably the greenhouse for me").

Size

As I had mentioned earlier, make sure you are aware of the kinds of plants and crops you intend to grow, as that essentially lets you know how big your greenhouse should be. If you are new to gardening but you are not sure how to begin, then get a small greenhouse. Beginners or casual gardeners who are uncertain if they would like to be long-term gardeners often imagine that they would like to get themselves a big greenhouse. They imagine that once they master their gardening techniques, they will already have a large enough space to work on more plants. But that is counterintuitive, and one should always consider space if they have decided to invest their time in raising plants. For one, greenhouses are expensive. You may not be using all the space available to you, but you still have to maintain it. Your best bet is to work with a small greenhouse in the beginning. Once you get comfortable cultivating crops, you can choose to invest in a bigger structure (or an expansion). One thing to note is that even if you are investing in a small greenhouse, it is still an investment, which is why I recommend getting a cold frame, which are essentially mini-greenhouses. They allow you to work with small plants and vegetables. Once you get used to them, you might think one of two thoughts:

- I think I am ready to invest more time for growing plants and crops. Bring in the big guns! Or in this case, the big greenhouses!

- I think I am comfortable with a cold frame and if I need to, I might just get myself a small greenhouse. They are easier to maintain and cost less!

Give it a thought and see what conclusions you draw.

GREENHOUSE GARDENING

Figure 4: Cold frame

Space

Since you are buying a greenhouse, draw a floor of the space available to you. Start marking the areas you are planning to use for gardening. Add spaces for movement. If you are planning to get a wheelbarrow, then you might prefer to have wider spaces. Give areas for potting benches, shelves, and even a storage unit. Once you have made the measurements, always add a little more space. This is important for two reasons:

- Your measurements (as with all measurements) may not be precise. Giving a little extra wiggle room allows you to adapt in case you run out of space.

- Gardens are often known to outgrow the greenhouse, so adding a little more space keeps you prepared in case you plan to add more plants during the year.

Frame

Use the "Frame Materials" section to find out just what material you want to use for the greenhouse frame. Here are a few questions that might help you pick the right frame:

- Do you prefer an inexpensive material? Try not to think of this question as a way to cut short on the quality of your frame. After all, you need to ponder upon future investments like a wheelbarrow, raised beds, or other materials you may require. If you feel that you have enough to go around for every item that you may require for your greenhouse, then feel free to spend on heavier frame materials.

- Would you like to work with a lightweight frame?

- How is the weather in your region? If the summers can get sufficiently hot, then you could invest in aluminum framing to retain more heat.

- Does it get windy in your region? If that is indeed the case, then perhaps having a frame that is too lightweight (such as plastic) might not be a viable option.

Cover

Use the section "Cover Materials" to find out more about the various cover options for your greenhouse. When choosing the right cover, think of the questions below:

- Do you have a lot of sunlight in your region? That could help you pick out a translucent material like polycarbonate. This becomes important in hot regions, because you require sufficient sunlight for your plants, but you do not want the intense sunlight of the region affecting your plant growth.

- Would you require a strong cover? This might be especially important in regions that suffer hail or snow (snow can add weight to the cover and cause it to bend.)

- What is your budget for cover? Can you pick one of the less expensive options?

I am certain that while you are choosing your frames and covers, you might find yourself asking questions that you probably might not have thought of before. Everything from the type of soil you have to the drainage facilities you are considering building might be essential for choosing the right materials. So do not be in a hurry. Take your time and make an informed decision.

Professional Greenhouse

With a professional greenhouse, you can grow multiple crops at one time. These greenhouses are tall, with some even reaching as high as twenty feet, and wide, with widths of more than forty feet. Professional greenhouses come equipped with roof ventilation systems, roll-up doors, and even grow lights, which are lights that are designed to provide the necessary heat for your plants whenever required (especially during the night or in winter). You can find these greenhouses with an NFT system (Nutrient Film Technique) that are useful for growing small crops. Inside these greenhouses, you might also find benches and wagons to transport materials from one end of the greenhouse to another (as they can be quite long).

You might not require a professional greenhouse for your gardening work. These greenhouses are meant for industries, large businesses, or as a public facility. However there are many options for you to choose from that provide you with space and the capacity to

GREENHOUSE GARDENING

work with numerous plants and crops.

Figure 5: A professional greenhouse

Commercial Greenhouses

These greenhouses are large and do require more space, but not as much as a professional greenhouse. You might not be using them in your own backyard (unless you have a large backyard, in which case, these greenhouses might work for you).

One of the things about a commercial greenhouse is that it provides you with sufficient space to get started. Once you have started with your initial plants and crops, you can decide to add more in the future. Addition of plants might not be a challenge, as you already have enough space to work with. You can look under the section "Designing and Building a Greenhouse" to understand some of the options that you can work with including the structure type, frame materials, and cover options.

Figure 6: A commercial greenhouse

Hobby Greenhouses

These are small greenhouses that you can erect in your backyard or even on the roof of a building. Often, you can purchase entire hobby greenhouse kits that come with the frame, cover and a few essential features. With hobby greenhouses, what you are essentially focusing on is growing plants, crops, or flowers at a time comfortable to you.

Figure 7: A hobby greenhouse

CHAPTER 3

GREENHOUSE ENVIRONMENT

Your greenhouse contains a climate of its own. Greenhouses have their own micro ecosystems that maintain heat, humidity, water, sunlight, nutrients, and other factors to ensure that the organisms within it grow properly. You have to take into consideration all these factors to ensure that the plants receive optimal growing conditions. As a matter of fact, you could say that you are modifying climatic conditions within a greenhouse to ensure proper growth of those plants.

This is why building (or buying) a greenhouse is just one part of the equation. You now have to consider maintaining a greenhouse all year long.

What do you do to ensure that you can have a greenhouse ready to grow crops any time of the year?

Seasons Greetings - Working With Greenhouse Seasons

The idea of year-round greenhouses is slowly becoming a popular concept. So what exactly is a year-round greenhouse? Do greenhouses disappear in the middle of the year or something if they are not year-round?

You do not have to worry about your greenhouse absconding anywhere. A year-round greenhouse refers to a greenhouse that is capable of producing crops at any time of the year. This is because of the introduction of improved technology, better fertilizers, and techniques that assist the gardener in keeping his or her plants healthy at any time of the year. This is also useful for people who would like to keep their produce going even during certain off-seasons.

Nowadays, greenhouses are becoming popular for producing home-grown ingredients regardless of the temperature outside. However, in order to reap the benefits of a good harvest, it is essential to plan ahead of time. This allows you to consider factors such as the types of crops that you would like to plant and the ideal conditions required for their growth.

GREENHOUSE GARDENING

If you have a long growing season, then you may begin planting your crops early. This also allows you to plant multiple rounds of crops. But do note that by doing this, you will have to subject the plants to the different climatic conditions, which might not be ideal for certain plants.

For example, let us take cold-season vegetables. These are plants that are capable of withstanding cold temperatures ranging between 53 degrees Fahrenheit to 70 degrees Fahrenheit. These plants are also capable of facing a small amount of frost. Some of the examples of plants that belong to the cold-season group are carrots, turnips, lettuces, peas, and potatoes.

On the other hand, you have warmer season plants that can survive in temperatures ranging from 64 degrees Fahrenheit to around 78 degrees Fahrenheit. You may find these plants unable to handle frost. Some of the plants that require warmer climates are eggplants, cucumbers, pumpkins, and beans.

When selecting the type of plant, you might have to consider how long a season will last. After all, you do not want your beans to freeze before you even have a chance to taste them! That would be a disaster.

So what can you do in such situations? Well, you can prepare your own microclimate.

Microclimates

There are some tricks that you can use to keep your plants healthy regardless of the season. Remember that these may not always work for every plant. I would ideally recommend trying to grow the right plant for the right season. Nevertheless, I understand trying to grow a plant in a season not fit for it. Who wants to wait until winter to enjoy some cucumbers, right?

Either ways, try out these techniques.

Grouping

Plants that can withstand cold temperatures are called "hardy plants," which is why you do not have to concern yourself with these plants during winter. However, for other plants (known as "tender" plants), you might find them struggling to make it through the cold. If only placing a blanket over them was the solution. But sadly, that is not the case, and these plants require a lot more care. What you can do is group these plants together. This makes them more resilient and even increases the humidity slightly, helping them withstand the dip in temperatures.

Mulch

Adding a layer of organic mulch helps in maintaining the soil temperature better. It also protects the soil from mild temperature fluctuations. Apart from temperature, you might also find that mulch retains moisture, assisting with the growth of your plants.

Wind blocks

Any surface such as a wall, fence, or even nearby buildings can act as protection against gusts of wind or even snow. When plants are close to these surfaces, they can leech onto the small amount of warmth that they provide. During summer, if your plants cannot stand the heat, you can use these surfaces as sun blocks.

Water

When plants are close to water, they tend to make use of the slight temperature moderating effects of the liquid. If you have sources of water close by, such as an artificial pool or a natural lake, then you can take advantage of the source. This become particularly useful during summertime for plants that cannot stand much heat.

It Is That Time Of The Season

While you cannot control seasons, you can definitely decide what kinds of plants to grow depending on the temperature outside. As I had mentioned earlier, planning is key. Crops fall into two categories. On one hand, you have the cool-season crops that are ideal for winter or fall. On the other hand, you have warm season crops that are perfect for summer or spring.

No matter what season it is, you can make use of it to get the most out of your gardening.

Cool Season Crops

For this season, you are looking at hardy plants or semi-hardy plants. If you plan to harvest your plants in spring, then you could think of planting them during early winter. If you would like to harvest them during fall, then your best bet is to plant your crops during late summer. If you would like to know the climate times, you can check your local climate and weather conditions online. With these cool season plants, you can get the best flavor if you allow them to mature under cool temperatures. Some of the cool season crops you can get started with are cabbage, kale, parsley, broccoli, spinach, leeks, and the ones we had mentioned above under "Greenhouse Seasons."

Warm Season Crops

You have entered spring or summer and you are wondering if there is any way to grow some delicious ingredients without worrying about the effects of the sun. Why, of course there is. Ideally, you should plant warm season crops during spring, when the threat of frost has long passed. This is because these crops are rather tender and might require you to maintain them between 65 degrees Fahrenheit to around roughly 90 degrees Fahrenheit (that is 18 degrees Celsius to 32 degrees Celsius for you for "degree C" folks). The reason for choosing this time is to allow them to have sufficient sunlight and to bask in the warmth of the summer (a mild sunbathing for our vegetable friends, so to speak). Some of the warm season crops that you can get started with are okra, tomatoes, melons, corn, and a few others that we covered under "Greenhouse Seasons."

Now that you know the different types of crops that you can grow, let us understand some science behind growing the crops in different climatic conditions. Onwards, my fellow gardener!

For Winter

Let's get started with the cold part of the year. What you should be looking for is the availability of natural sunlight. As we had seen earlier, you should always seek to find places that provide you with enough sunlight. This is essential for growing crops, regardless of the climate you face (as winter typically provides less sunlight.) Another factor that you should take into consideration for winter specifically is the natural outdoor temperature.

Should you have a deficiency of both of the above factors (that is, proper sunlight and the right temperature), then you can always make use of artificial lighting. Getting UV lamps is an effective way to do this. However, make sure you have the right UV scale. You do not want your plants to turn out deep fried!

But the above method is a last ditch effort. You see, the main purpose of having a greenhouse is to make use of natural light, heat, and temperature conditions for your plants.

To understand the ways in which you can make use of winter for your crops, it is important to get started with the science behind how plants make use of natural conditions.

You might be aware of the basics. Plants essentially convert carbon dioxide into oxygen. They also utilize water that they absorb through the roots and disperse through their leaves in a process called "transpiration." This water is the source of a number of nutrients for the plants. That is one reason why it is important to pay attention to this water consumption cycle of the plants when you have an artificial system for growing crops.

When there is an excess of humidity within the greenhouse, then it gets too dry for the plants. This prevents them from transpiring water fast enough. This adds stress to the plants, and they eventually begin to rot.

Different winter plants are used to different levels of humidity. However, when you typically consider plants that thrive during winter, then you are looking at those plants that receive the right temperature and the right levels of humidity. This means that while sunlight is necessary, it is the ability to control the flow of air, the temperature levels inside the greenhouse, and the water supply to the plants that matters.

Here are a few ways you can keep conditions during winter ideal for plant growth.

Temperature

This is an important factor for controlling humidity. What you should be ideally looking for is to utilize the low-level temperatures and find crops that grow in such conditions. Raising the temperature, while it may sound convenient, is rather counterintuitive, especially considering the electricity bill you might receive at the end of the month! However, if it is truly necessary, you can induce artificial lighting to grow certain plants. I would recommend you make use of the season rather than establishing alternatives in your greenhouse.

Airflow

Getting the right flow of air depends on ventilation. With the right air flow, you might be able to manage the humidity in your greenhouse. Make use of the vents in your greenhouse (if you have not considered adding vents to your greenhouse, then take this part as a note to do so) to induce a nice airflow. Adding exhaust fans to your greenhouse might also help you improve the conditions. An ideal way to go about constructing vents is to use this technique.

- Make sure that you place your exhaust fans near the edge of the ceiling.

- Then, place intake vents near the floor of the greenhouse.

This arrangement is useful to remove the damp interior air outside and allow in drier air. Why does dry air flow through the intake vents at the floor? That is simple; warm air rises and cold air settles down.

Keeping the intake vents at the bottom give you access to this cold, dry air. By keeping the exhaust fan at the top, you are removing the warm air from the greenhouse. If you are wondering why we are removing the wet air from the greenhouse, then you should know that damp air is the reason for humidity. We are simply removing humidity by getting to the root of the problem.

Water

A very essential factor. Also, one that is quite overlooked, surprisingly. Water is useful to control the humidity of the greenhouse. I can probably imagine what some of you are thinking. Hold on! You just removed damp air, but you chose to keep water? What changed? Here is the thing. I am not talking about keeping water around. Rather, I am talking about supplying water to the plants. You see, despite the measures that we take to remove humidity, it always leaves an effect on your plants. Hence, ensure that you have a proper supply of water to your soil, giving the roots of the plants some much-needed nutrients.

With that, you are ready to grow crops during the winter.

For Summer

Summer! The season for chilled drinks, trips to the beach, and of course, growing some incredible crops. What we are focusing on is the idea of getting your plants ready to face the heat.

Let us establish a basic fact; if you are growing cacti or certain types of succulents, then you do not have to worry too much about these plants. They are well suited to handle the heat waves during summer. However, their ability to handle the heat comes with a caveat. They are not used to handling the heat waves indoors. Which means, you need to figure out what to do for these plants in your lovely greenhouse.

The first think that you should do is to find out when summer might possibly hit your region. Keep an eye out for weather forecasts and see if there is the possibility of any extreme heat waves.

Once you have all the necessary information, here is what you need to do.

Humidity

No, you will not have to control the humidity this time. In fact, you need to induce more humidity. Summer plants love this, and it helps them grow healthy. Here is a pro tip. Fill up a small bowl or a dish with pebbles. Next, add water to the container, and keep this next to the plants. If you are growing crops directly on the ground, then keep the container next to the plants. If you are raising plants inside a raised bed, then keep the container below the raised bed, if you have space for that. The sun heats up the water and turns in into water vapor. With water vapor in the air, you can artificially induce humidity. This technique will provide your plants their own little microclimate. Nifty, isn't it?

Water

You should replace the water that escapes. Which is why the key thing to remember is that you have to water well and water regularly. Since it is summer, plants need to hydrate and seek out nutrients faster. The heat from the sun can cause the water from the soil to evaporate quicker, which is why your water supply should be ideal for the plant. If you water too fast (or if you do not provide enough water), the top of the soil ends up getting more water. The rest of the water simply flows down the sides and ends up wasted. Take your time to water the plants during summer. Make sure that water is not escaping down the sides. If you notice water being wasted, slow down on how much you supply to the plants.

Make sure you check soil moisture regularly. You can either use a handy moisture meter to do this, or you could use a free tool - your finger! Simply place your finger in the soil, ideally to a depth of two inches, and see if you feel moisture. If you do not, it's time to get watering.

Typically, you might be able to see visual cues of plants that do not receive enough water. Some plants tend to wilt, while others encounter scorched leaves. You might also notice young foliage drying out. If you notice these factors, make sure that you supply water to the plants immediately.

Apart from the above steps, also make sure that you are performing the below actions:

Ventilation

For the summer, make sure you have sufficient roof ventilation. This will allow the hot air (which rises) to escape the greenhouse while you have a nice layer of cool air settling at the bottom. You could also keep a thermometer inside the greenhouse or with you to check the temperature inside the greenhouse frequently. Some crops can handle temperatures above 81 degrees Fahrenheit (roughly 27 degrees Celsius.) However, for those plants that cannot handle high heat, make sure ventilation is available to them.

Shading

One thing to note about trying to shade your plants is that they depend on sunlight. You can use blinds to give a nice amount of shade. You can add these blinds to the exterior or interior of the greenhouse. However, choose an option that makes it convenient for you to remove them when necessary. You could also have the feature of attaching blinds that can slide open or closed. This might involve a little more expense from your end, but it adds more convenience. If you prefer to spend less, then you could make use of meshes or nettings to give a nice cover for your plants. Do note that for some of these meshes and nets, you might have to hold them in place using clips or other methods.

Dampness

Here is a cool trick to raise the humidity level in your greenhouse. If you have cobblestones or stone paths inside your greenhouse, then you know that they tend to heat up and that heat radiates upwards (hot air rising). This causes them to heat the plants. To avoid this, you can simply hose down the path or pour water on it. This not only cools the path, minimizing heat radiation, but also allows the water to evaporate. When water evaporates, it creates a nice humidity level for the plants. Now that's science for you!

For Spring

One of the things that you can do during spring (and practically any other time of the year) is add compost to your soil.

This is a useful addition because it creates healthy and long-lasting soil. Additionally, it maintains the pH levels of the soil, gives the roots nutrients, and makes the soil ideal for planting. However, here is a tip I think would come in handy for you. Try to use cover crops, which are special crops that you can use to enrich and protect the soil. The way they work is that when you plant them, their roots dig into the soil and mixes up the essential nutrients. This is why, when you are in need of essential nutrients, you can simply plant these crops at the beginning of spring. By the time you harvest them, you will have soil rich in wonderful nutrients for your warm-season plants to enjoy.

You could also use certain quick cover crops that you can harvest in a short period of time. This allows you to grow the rest of your plants in the same season. First, check the weather and make sure that the temperature is not extreme. Then go ahead and plant these cover crops. A few examples of these crops are oats, barley, and mustard. These crops provide you with essential organic materials for the vegetables and plants that you would like to grow later. A popular crop for cover has been ryegrass, but it is known to return during the summer as a stubborn weed (removing it is a cumbersome process). Your next alternative would be to use mustard, but make sure you get yourself high quality plants. Mustard is known to harbor diseases that can harm other plants, though humans are safe from this.

For Autumn/Fall

The one thing you should ensure before growing any crops during autumn or fall is to take out any crops that are not growing well. If you notice crops wilting away or showing signs of poor quality, simply remove them for other plants. Check the soil for weeds and make sure you add in compost to set the soil.

A good tip to follow is to make use of all the leftover seeds from spring. Always use a high-quality compost and make sure you clean out your containers. This is particularly important to clean out unwanted organisms that might be lying around.

However, if you live in a region that typically enjoys hot climates and has no autumn/fall, then you might as well get started with cool-season crops.

CHAPTER 4

PROTECTING YOUR GREENHOUSE

Gone With The Wind - Wind Protection

Wind. When it gets too powerful, your plants might feel the effects of it.

If you have a greenhouse that has a sturdy structure or is built using strong cover materials, your plants might have good resistance against the wind. However, if you are using materials like plastic sheeting, then you might have a fair degree of trouble from winds.

This does not mean that you should change the materials (which could be an expensive endeavor) or avoid using inexpensive materials for your greenhouse (again, could involve getting costlier materials. Also, have faith in me fellow gardener. There is always a solution).

So what does one do against such strong gusts of wind? We could use the techniques mentioned earlier to give protection to your plants against snow and wind.

The first thing that you should be doing is getting as much information as possible about when strong winds typically appear in your area. You might already know about these timings yourself, or you could seek out the help of someone. Either way, it helps to be prepared.

The next factor you should consider is finding out if there are any nearby structures or objects that are blocking your plants from the wind. For example, do you have a building protecting your plants? This will help you know how best to protect your greenhouse. Additionally, knowing the arrangement of buildings nearby will give you an understanding of a "wind tunnel." Sometimes, when your greenhouse is placed between buildings, you will notice a gust of wind blowing in one direction. The direction usually does not change, depending on the layout of the buildings. That is essentially a wind tunnel. You can use the knowledge of a wind tunnel to set up barriers accordingly.

Staking

One of the things that you can do is stake the plants. This process secures the plants to a surface, ensuring that they do not feel the effects of strong winds. This might bend the plants slightly, but the winds do no uproot the plants entirely.

Height

In some areas, people have developed unique methods to protect their plants from the winds. Many gardeners alternate between high plants and low plants. By doing this, they allow the tall plants to provide protection for the smaller ones. You do not have to group them together very close. Having slight spacing between the plants allows the short ones to receive ample shield from the taller ones.

Raised Beds

A big problem that strong winds cause is that they easily erode the soil. This happens when winds brush away some of the topsoil, leaving the roots of the plants exposed to the elements. Consider planting on raised beds rather than directly into the soil. When using a raised bed, ensure that the fencing of the bed is high enough to protect the bases of the plants. The wind might still blow against the plants, but it won't carry any of the soil away. In fact, the soil might move around within the raised bed, which is alright as there is no real loss of soil.

Pest Control - Managing Pests

The term pest control often conjures up images of people using sprays filled with chemicals. You might think that using such methods is rather extreme. But if you spot your wonderful tomatoes surrounded by ants or your beautiful flowers suddenly attacked by flies, then you might think of drowning those creatures in pesticides.

However, what might sound like a frightening scenario can typically be solved by taking a few precautionary steps. If all else fails and you still would like to consider using sprays, then do not worry. I have a section to help you use them effectively.

The thing about pesticides is that they have an instant (and noticeable) effect. You can see the number of pests on your plants reduced. Nevertheless, there are certain effects in the long term – such as depleting the health of your soil and slightly poisoning your water – that might prove disastrous for you in the future. You might have to change the soil entirely. If you are using a raised bed, then this might not be a problem. However, if you have decided to plant directly into the earth, then getting rid of all that pesticide residue is a strenuous process.

Here is another thing that you should keep in mind; sometimes, getting rid of the pests may not be necessary. If you have aphids roaming around on your plants, then see if you have helpful insects that dine on these aphids. In fact, certain farmers are known to let the pests live. This is because they usually have some form of predator that can take care of the pest problem. This has two beneficial results:

- You do not have to spend time (and money, in some situations) on pest control activities.

- You let someone (or something) else take care of the problem for you. A friend in need is a friend indeed. Even if that friend just happens to have four legs, wings, or antennae.

Another thing to keep in mind; your problem might not be related to pests. It is easy to think that certain creatures have wreaked havoc on your lovely garden. Actually, it is certainly tempting to think that way. However, in many cases, the situation might just be because of other factors. Is there enough moisture for the plants? Are strong winds causing harm to them? Was there heavy rainfall recently? Did it hail? Even water pollution could be another factor to consider. You see, all of these factors cause unnecessary stress on the plants, which further begins to attract the pests in your area. Trying to get to the root of the problem might help you effectively remove the pests without using any pest control techniques (including pesticides).

The idea behind evaluating your garden is to know what kind of problem you are dealing with. That may help you decide if you would like to head over to the next step, which is the integrated pest management, or 'IPM' for short, process.

In IPM, farmers and gardeners take gradually stronger steps to get rid of the pests in their garden. They start by working on the conditions that help the growth of the crops. Are these conditions beneficial? Do the crops have everything they need? Once they are able to work around these conditions, they seek to establish a level of damage they can accept. Once that is done, they move on to using methods that have minimal toxicity. If that does not work, they begin using toxic or invasive methods.

Join the Resistance!

The first thing that you should do is focus on creating pest resistance plants. You see, gardeners and farmers often work with a plethora of plants species. Some of these plants have some unique traits. One of those unique traits is the ability of the plant to have disease resistance. This means that the plant suffers minimal damage from a specific disease, similar to how the human immune system builds resistances against diseases.

Many of the modern plants have built resistance to many diseases that could cause considerable damage. What's more, you can find plants that also have resistance to certain insects. For example, you can find special types of squash that can keep away certain types of beetles. This might help you effectively find a solution against these pests without having to resort to other methods of pest control.

In fact, when you are purchasing plants, you might receive information about what pests those plants resist. After knowing what pests are common in your area, you can match the plant to that particular pest.

Inviting Less Pests

While you might be confident that you have taken all the precautionary steps to keep away pests, there might be certain reasons your garden is still attracting those nasty critters.

Plant Conditions

Make sure you have placed the plant in the right spot, based on how much water, sunlight, and essential nutrients that the plant may require. This is because stress begins to affect those plants that do not receive what they require. The stress in turn causes plants to release certain chemicals in the air, which are like beacons for all the pests in the area. Humans might deal with stress through many means. Plants however, do not have mechanisms to resist stress. They eventually begin to experience deteriorating health and finally succumb to the effects of pests. This does not mean that healthy plants cannot attract pests, but they are capable of surviving attacks when an unhealthy plant may not be able to.

Mixed Plants

Most insects have receptors that allow them to target their favorite plants. It is how bees can seek out nectar so easily. If you have the plants that insects are waiting to attack and you have done nothing to protect those plants, then you might as well schedule buffet hours for the insects! What you can do to avoid this situation is to plant your crops in small batches throughout your garden. Then you can add other plants into the mix (preferably those that have resistance against the pests in your area). This confuses the insects, tricking them into believing that perhaps your garden does not have the food they are looking for. Additionally, you might be able to avoid diseases from spreading when you mix plant breeds.

Timing

Certain pests often arrive during certain climates. This fact might give you an idea of the kind of threat you are dealing with. When plants are young, they do not have the strength to ward off pests effectively, which is why you can plant your crops early so that by the time pest climate arrives, your crops have strong tissues. In some cases, insects often leave eggs behind in gardens. When the larvae hatch, they find a ready source of food in the plants around them. For this reason, you could also plant your crops a few weeks after the larvae have hatched, allowing you to starve the pests before working on your garden.

Here is a pro tip: speak to farmers in your area about the emergence of pests. They have extensive knowledge about when these pests might come out during a particular season, allowing you to know how long to wait before planting your crops.

Crop Rotation

You can move around the crops to new locations in your greenhouse each year. This does not give pests a particular spot to target. Shifting locations confuses the pests, who might be used to finding plants in a specific spot of the garden. Certain insects often lay their eggs in one location when they realize that they know where they can find a ready supply of food. However, by moving your crops around, larvae that hatch might not find their food source. Before they can discover food, they might starve and you might be able to get rid of them without much effort. Do note that crop rotation is most commonly possible with annual plants, when they can be cycled year after year. Perennial plants are usually harvested after one year, so they cannot be quickly rotated. So make a note of this when you plan to change plant locations in your garden. More on annual and perennial plants in Chapter 10.

Go Easy on the Fertilizer

This might be a common mistake committed by beginners. Gardeners who are starting out might worry about the amount of fertilizer that they use. Many use too much to avoid using too little. Unfortunately, too much fertilizer can cause harm to plants, just the way too little can. In fact, you could say that increasing the amount of fertilizer to a plant is like giving steroids to them! For example, soil nutrients provide nitrogen to the plant. This is good in moderate quantities. By adding more fertilizer, you increase the supply of nitrogen. Providing excess amounts of nitrogen might cause rapid growth in plants. This causes them to end up being juicy. This might not sound all that bad. Who doesn't love juicy food? You and every other multi-legged creature will be waiting to get a bite out of those plants. Pests might become attracted to the unnatural growth, finding a rich source of food for them and their offspring.

Clean Up Other Materials

If you notice fallen leaves, fruits, or other objects in your garden that should not typically be there, then make sure you clear them out. These objects and debris might carry organisms and pests on them that could be transferred to your plants. This increases the chances of infecting your plants with diseases or sending pests into their midst. Once you have cleaned up, see if you can also cultivate the soil when you get the opportunity. This reveals any hidden pest eggs. Additionally, if there are any larvae, you might just let predators (or even the weather) get rid of them.

Make Friends With Creatures

I am not asking you to invite creatures into your house for tea and supper. What I mean is to allow the growth of certain organisms that could help you get rid of pests. For example, certain types of spiders leave your plants alone, but find abundant food in the pests that might live there. You can always encourage the growth of these pest-hunters, as you can call them.

Identifying Dangers

No matter how experienced you become at gardening, there is no avoiding pests. If you have a plant growing in your garden, chances are that there is a pest out there waiting to pounce upon it.

What you should do is try and identify these pests. If you step into your garden one day and notice a spider or a group of ants on your plants, it does not mean that they immediately should be classified as pests. They might just have wandered into your colorful ecosystem looking for food. Get in touch with local farmers or perform your own research into finding out what creatures you should recognize as a threat and what organisms are safe. This way, you leave out the creatures who can help you and target those whom you don't recall sending an invite to attend your garden.

The next thing you should do after identifying a pest is to assess your plant for damage. It is easy to enter panic mode because, let's face it, pests are generally disgusting and you never know if they have laid any eggs or not. Which is why you should take your time to check the plants for possible damage. Are the leaves affected, or do you notice problems on the entire plant? Do you spot any discoloration? If so, is this discoloration spreading all over the plant or just restricted to a specific area? Has this infection or attack affected nearby plants as well?

Then it is time to look at the plant more closely. Check those areas that you wouldn't usually, like the bottom of leaves or the area where leaves meet stems. What you are doing right now is looking for traces of eggs, small insects, or organisms. Check the way these organisms or eggs are clustered. Make sure you approach the plant with care. You might frighten off these pests. While that might sound like a solution, it only scares them away for a short duration before they return. During this process, you are simply trying to find a pattern to their movement and organization. Return at different times of the day and watch the pests. If you are lucky, you might catch them in action, which helps you gain a better understanding about them. As you are gaining more information about the pests, keep making notes. You might need them later on for reference.

Using the above information, you can find out how to get rid of the pests while dealing the least amount of damage to your plants.

Knowing How To Deal With Your Pest

Here is where the information you gathered comes into play. Without the information, you might think that you need to act quickly and get rid of the pests. Time to bring in the big guns! However, what you should be doing is analyzing the situation properly. Do you see pests restricted to a particular plant or spreading out in your garden? Even if these creatures are spread out, do you notice them in few numbers or do you see hundreds of them?

This process is known as establishing damage thresholds. It basically means that you are trying to measure the extent of pest growth in your garden before taking reactive measures.

If you have a small number of pests, then you can think about using one of the solutions provided below. However, if the pests have multiplied to a considerable amount, then it might be the time to introduce the big guns (and by that, I mean pesticides).

Choose Your Control Method

After getting the necessary information and concluding how severe the pest problem is, you can choose various control methods to deal with the problem.

Physical Control Methods

If pests are getting to your crops, then you could try physically keeping them away. There are a number of ways to do this. Here are a few:

Erecting Barriers

Call this your initial defense plan. By setting up barriers, you can prevent pests from actually reaching your plants. A good example could be a fence, which are great for keeping away rodents and animals such as cats (yes, our feline friends can be pests, too). To protect against birds, you could use bird netting. Wire meshes and other forms of netting may be able to protect your crops from flying insects. When you become aware of what insect or animal causes your garden a lot of distress, you can choose an appropriate physical barrier.

Getting Handy

Many farmers and gardeners simply choose to use their hands to pick away the pests, if those pests are large bugs and creatures such as snails. This is an inexpensive and a non-toxic method of getting rid of your creature problem. However, if you feel squeamish about working with your hands, there are many bug vacuums on the market to help you do the job.

Using Water

If you discover small creatures inhabiting your garden without your permission, then you can easily get rid of them with a spray or stream of water. Simply bring your hose to your plants, turn on the water and dislodge these nasty critters. In addition to removing pests, you end watering the plants as well. However, do make sure that you do not use a lot of water. You might end up drowning the plants.

Adding Repellants

You can also utilize certain substances that pests do not come close to. For your typical garden pests, you can make use of special oils or scents. Look for any repellant that matches the pest that is currently attacking your garden. Oh, and by the way, by repellant, I don't mean a bug repellant! That's a pesticide (which we will cover in a section further in the book).

Creating Traps

Traps work well because they are unexpected. They are designed to either lure a creature towards it or catch them unaware. A common example is the spring loaded trap for catching mice. There are numerous traps for different scenarios, such as glue traps, electronic traps, and more. Find the one that suits your needs.

Biological Control Methods

Under these control methods, you are using a living organism to take care of the more dangerous organisms in your garden. Typically, this would mean using creatures beneficial to your garden (as we had seen some examples earlier). However, in this case, we are also considering substances that have useful bacteria or fungi that we can apply on the plants. These substances have a repelling effect. They prevent the pest from approaching your plants.

GREENHOUSE GARDENING

Other Control Methods

You can make use of a range of pesticides that are available in the market. Use them when you know that there are no other options left to you and that using any of the above methods does not solve the problem. When you are looking for pesticides, know that there a few kinds of them.

Insecticides

These are a form of pesticide that are specifically made to harm, eliminate, or repel one or more species of insect. You can discover insecticides in various forms such as sprays, gels, and even traps. Pick one based on the pest that is attacking your garden.

Once you have selected your insecticide, it is better to know the below tips:

- I would recommend using just one type of insecticide in your garden. Adding two or more insecticides diminishes their effect and may inadvertently cause harm to your garden.

- Remember that not all insecticides take the same time to remove pests from your garden. You might have to wait longer for certain types.

- Try to see if you really need the spray. For

example, if you want to get rid of ants, you could use a bait instead (after all, ants are attracted to nearby sources of food).

Fungicides

These are pesticides that are made to kill fungal infections on the plants and any fungi spores that might have latched onto your crops. In some cases, fungicides are used to mitigate the effects of mildew and mold. The way they function is by damaging either the fungal cell structure or stopping the energy production in cells.

When you are ready to use your fungicide, do make note of the below tips:

- In many cases, people might accidently diagnose fungal diseases for their plants when in reality, it might not be a disease at all. Make sure you use the help of local experts to give you a second opinion. They might just prevent you from buying a fungicide needlessly and might recommend another solution.

- Make sure that leaves are not kept wet for too long. Simply keeping the leaves dry after watering them helps reduce the spread of fungi.

- Keep your tools sanitized. Sometimes, the

fungi could spread from one plant to another because they stuck to the tools you were using.

Herbicides

The main purpose of herbicides in a garden is to get rid of all the weeds.

When you have gotten your herbicide, do make note of the following tips:

- Always make sure that the instructions on the herbicide suit your purposes.

- Go easy on its application. Adding more herbicide might sound like a safe bet, but it might end up damaging your plants. If you feel unsure, read the instructions provided on the herbicide to understand its usage quantity.

- Certain herbicides show immediate results. Others take a while to get rid of the weeds. Always check with the seller or supplier for details before using the herbicide. This way, you are not left wondering if you had bought a defective product when you see weeds present even after the third day of using the herbicide.

- Herbicides also have an effect on the soil, so make sure you speak to experts about your garden's soil types before you make a purchase.

Center For Disease Control - Protecting Against Diseases

Nothing is as frustrating as knowing that you have gotten your plants protected against the elements and nasty critters, only to find that they have now caught a nasty bug. And by that, I don't mean the ones that crawl (for the crawlers, please refer to section "Pest Control"). I am referring those bugs that are microscopic and capable of such macroscopic harm. I am, of course, referring to diseases.

As the saying goes, "Prevention is better than a cure." That is true in this case as well, which is why I will include some preventive measures that you can take to keep those diseases at bay.

Maintain Soil Health

Always keep an eye on your soil. I had mentioned using the right fertilizer, making sure you water the crops properly, and other techniques to keep your soil healthy. By following these tips, you might be able to prevent diseases affecting your soil and spreading into your roots.

The foundation of any good plant is it its root (both

literally and figuratively), which is why you need to make sure you establish a strong foundation.

Two of the most essential criteria to follow to keep the soil healthy are:

- Make sure you feed your plants. This means providing them with the essential nutrients while also supplying adequate water.

- Look out for pests that are capable of spreading diseases. Leafhoppers are a type of insect known to spread diseases caused by viruses. In this scenario, you should focus on pest control. Find out more information about the pest and eliminate them using any of the steps mentioned earlier under "Pest Control."

Remove Mildew

Mildew is the term used to name airborne fungal diseases that tend to leave a layer of white powdery substances on garden plants. If you spot such powdery deposits on your plants, then make sure you get rid of them as soon as you can. Wait too long, and the substance can dry out your plant, turning their leaves brown and killing the plant itself.

In this scenario, you might think of using fungicides. That is a completely normal reaction. However, your plants host essential fungi as well, which help the plant in many ways. So killing one kind of fungi means getting rid of the useful ones.

The alternative is to use a method that is less toxic.

Firstly, got some milk? Not for drinking.

You see, all you need is a combination of milk and water. You can add one-fourth portion milk and the remaining portion should be water.

Spray that milk on the areas that are affected by the fungus on a sunny day, preferably in the morning. Spray on both sides of the leaves until you see the solution dripping. While scientists are still figuring out why milk removes mildew, farmers have widely begun to use this technique.

Drip Irrigation

One of the best forms of irrigation is drip irrigation. Not only do you get to save a lot of water through this method (you can waste more than 40% water using a sprinkler system), but you can also prevent your leaves from getting wet, which could potentially attract diseases in the future.

However, I know that you cannot completely avoid using sprinklers, as it all depend on how you would like to grow your garden. If you have to use sprinklers, then I recommend timing your sprinkler system. Once you spray water on the plants, let the leaves dry before sprinkling water on them again.

Protection Detail - Keeping Yourself Protected

While engaged in the process of taking care of your greenhouse, do not forget an important element in all of this; you.

After all, you are the most essential factor responsible for making sure that everything in your greenhouse runs smoothly.

Here are a few tips I recommend you follow when you are using the various techniques to protect your garden.

- Make sure your arms and legs are covered properly. Use long sleeved shirts or tops when handling pesticides or pests.

- Wear shoes when you step into your greenhouse. Make sure you have a pair meant only for use in your garden.

- Cover your head using a hat or a hairnet, especially when you are using pesticides. Your scalp tends to absorb chemicals, and that does not have a good result.

- Wear protective gloves whenever you are in the greenhouse. In fact, make it a habit to wear gloves. This not only protects you and the plant, but also keeps your hands relatively clean.

- When you are using pesticides, dealing with fungi, or clearing out debris, make sure you are covering your eyes. Do not rely on glasses. Get yourself goggles that cover your entire eye.

- Your lungs are fragile, and they need to be taken care of properly. Get yourself a mask to cover your nose. If you are able to, use respirators whenever you are dealing with pesticides.

CHAPTER 5

ESSENTIAL GREENHOUSE EQUIPMENT

Getting together the right tools and equipment for the job is a satisfying endeavor. Not only do you get to take pleasure in the fact that you are getting everything ready to begin your gardening adventure, but you are also mentally ticking off all the tools you might need to work with your plants. Think of it like a chef preparing his or her equipment to create your masterpiece.

In this case, your garden is your masterpiece.

I will mention many of the essential tools that you might require in gardening. However, with new technologies out there, you are never short of discovering a more convenient tool. Should you choose to pick any tool that provides you with some incredible features, do make note of the fact that it should fit your purposes. I have listed various tools below, but you do not need to get all of them (although it might be tempting). Think of what tool fits the purpose of your garden and get that one. You can always add tools in the future based on your requirements.

So let us go right ahead and start with some digging!

Digging Tools

Shovel/Spade

I always recommend having a shovel or a spade. These are versatile tools that allow you to work with your soil comfortably. If you head over to the local store, you may find a wide assortment of shovels, each with their own unique design and uses. However, generally speaking, you can use two main types of tools for digging; shovel and spades.

You might find people interchanging the names of shovel and spade to refer to the same tool. However, there is a noticeable difference between a shovel and a spade. And it all comes down to their shape.

If the tool has a round edge, then you are looking at a

shovel. With the rounded tip, you can dig into soil easily. I would suggest that you get a shovel that has a dish able to hold enough dirt.

If you notice that your tool has square edges, then you are looking at a spade. You can use this tool for lifting and throwing aside materials with relative ease. You can also use a spade to pat down the soil after distributing manure. This evens out the soil layer for you.

The type of tool you might require depends on how you plan to work in your garden.

Figure 8: A spade. With a shovel, you might get a rounded edge.

Trowel

Think of this tool as a mini spade. You might have seen this used in construction whenever there is a requirement for spreading cement or mortar. It has a similar purpose in gardening. Essentially, you can use the trowel for flattening soil and giving it an even layer. Additionally, you can dig up materials that you cannot otherwise with a shovel.

That does not mean that a shovel does not have enough strength to lift or break materials. It just means that sometimes, a shovel or a spade has a far reach. With that reach, you might not be able to make small adjustments to your garden wherever required.

Forks

No, not that ones you use to scoop up spaghetti. We are talking about garden forks. While it is not typically used in a garden, its use in digging tasks makes it a must-have in your greenhouse. What you cannot accomplish with a shovel and spade, you can with the garden fork. You simply have to hit this tool into the soil and using the handle's pullback mechanism to easily loosen the soil. This becomes useful when you are trying to remove crops.

Cultivating tools

When someone mentions the word cultivating, most people imagine a large farmland with a tractor and perhaps some cows. There is a connection there, so you are not entirely wrong. However, cultivating refers to the act of fertilizing the soil and removing any unnecessary weeds.

As you can see, this is an important role and requires the right tool to make it easier for you to get the cultivation done properly.

Hoes

As with all tools, you can get your hands on a variety of hoes. The options might befuddle you, but you just have to remember one essential criteria to having the right hoe: get one that allows you to both pull and push. Apart from that, do note some of the below tips to point you in the direction of the right kind:

You are not looking for a lightweight tool. Despite what some products might boast about (they are so light, it is like feather), go for one that is sturdy and strong. This is because you are probably going to be using a lot of effort while working with these tools. You do not want to get one that might break easily.

Next, you are also looking to get one that is sharp. When you push the tool, it has to cut into the soil easily.

Weeder

For those annoying weeds that never seem to go away, you now have a weapon of choice! Often, you might come across weeds that are hard to remove. With the weeder, you can deal with such weeds one at a time.

As with all tools, you might have no shortage of choice. However, what you should be looking for is a weeder that can work with the plants you are growing. If you are unable to decide, always ask for assistance with an expert or the supplier.

Cutting Tools

It is not always about just getting the sharpest tool in the shed. What you are looking for are tools that help you get specific tasks done. Here are some of the tools that you might require for your garden.

Pruners

You might notice that most gardeners always have pruners with them whenever they step out into a garden. What makes this tool so important?

For one, you can perform numerous tasks including snipping off the stems of plants that you have already harvested, cutting flowers after growing them, trimming plants and shrubs, and more.

When selecting a pruner, you need to look for one that has a comfortable handle. At the same time, you should also make sure that it is lightweight. This is because heavy pruners tend to add pressure to your hands, eventually causing discomfort in the long run.

Additionally, look for pruners that have carbon steel blades. This is for the sake of durability. Other forms of material chip away easily and you might find yourself bringing in a whetstone to sharpen the blade.

Check out the safety mechanisms of the pruner. A poor quality one might have weak springs. With weak springs, you might find yourself struggling as the spring cannot hold the pivot together. This causes the pruner to provide resistance, which makes using the tool rather uncomfortable.

Hedge Shears

Another marvelous tool for you to have. Essentially, you are look at a giant scissor-like object. They are used for cutting items and materials that you might not be able to otherwise cut using a pruner (since they are quite small, after all).

When you are looking for a hedge shear, make sure that you are looking for one that has a cushioned grip. If you have seen a shear in action, then you know that people use both hands, one on each handle provided, to work with the tool. You need something that is comfortable enough to not add unnecessary pressure on your palms.

The blade itself has to be long and sharp. There is no point in getting short-bladed hedge shears. You might as well save the money and make use of the pruner.

Lopper

Visually, a lopper is like the older, and taller, brother of the pruner. While the blades of both the pruner and the lopper have more or less the same dimensions, the handle is where the difference can be noticed. In a lopper, the handle is longer. This allows you to get into hard-to-reach places.

When looking for a lopper, make sure you get a sturdy handle preferably made out of hardwood or steel. You should also look for rubber handles that allow you a firm and comfortable grip.

Pruning Saw

Finally, when you need to get rid of stubborn stems or weeds that need more than just clippings from pruners, shears, or loppers, then you have the pruning saw.

A lot of people actually end up borrowing a pruning saw from someone else. I do not recommend it. Firstly, the tool itself is not expensive, so you are better off getting a new one. Secondly, you need a pruning saw that is ideal for your garden, so do not look for replacements. Finally, the quality that you get from tools that are borrowed is questionable at best.

CHAPTER 6

PLANT PROPAGATION

What is Plant Propagation?

When you need an inexpensive method for growing new plants, consider plant propagation. It is the technique by which you can use your old plants to start growing new ones. When you first start propagating plants, you might not be rewarded easily. It is a learning process, so it might take a few tries to get it right. However, do not lose hope. You will be able to get a hang of the technique through proper practice.

Many gardeners propagate plants using ideal conditions and materials like the right type of soil, special minerals for the roots, fertilizers, weather conditions, and other factors. They might not use water at all. But you can make use of water for propagating plants. Do make sure that you are certain that a particular plant can propagate in water. There are plants that can only make use of soil conditions.

I am going to show you a simply process by which you can propagate plants.

Step 1

Take your plant and look at the spot below the leaf or near the stem. You might be able to find a small brown root or protrusion. If you cannot discover one, look under other leaves. When you find this brown root, you need to make a cut an inch or two below it. This ensures that you include a big portion of the stem or leaf along with the protrusion.

Step 2

You are now going to put this brown root under water, so make sure that you remove any leaf too close to the root. This way, you should only have the root underwater. Any leaf should stay above water.

Step 3

Place your root in a glass or container of water. Next, place this container in an area that receives sunlight. Here is a tip: do not place the root under direct sunlight. This might affect the process. What you should do is find a place of moderate sunlight.

Step 4

This is probably the most important step. You need to be patient. Keep checking the root to make sure that there is progress. Change water when you see it getting discolored. My recommendation is to replace the water every couple or few days. Prevent the water from getting murky and check for any fungi.

Pretty soon, you might begin to notice the brown root growing into a separate plant.

However, the propagation technique that you just read about above is called "cutting." There are other ways to propagate a plant, which we will see below.

Seed Propagation

This is a popular method used by many gardeners. Many plants utilize seeds to grow. Hence, farmers or gardeners remove the seeds from the plants they want to propagate. The parent plant transfers its genetic markup (or genetic information) to its seeds. This way, using the seeds will allow you to grow the same plant again.

When you are working on the process of seed propagation, you first place the seeds in a small container (with water) until you start to notice small seedlings. Upon the arrival of the seedlings, simply transfer them to soil for further growth.

Cloning

Plant cloning is exactly as the name suggest; you replicate the plant to create multiple copies of it. While the whole idea of cloning might sound complex, the entire process is fairly easy to work with. Simply follow the below steps to clone a plant.

Step 1

The first thing that you need to do is select a healthy plant. Ideally, you should look for plants that are not affected by disease or do not have any fungi on them. Now you have to look for a branch that separates from the main stem. Look for the best one among the branches that you have, keeping an eye out for traits such as the branch health and color.

Step 2

Now you are going to cut the plant. Make sure that your tool has been sanitized. Any traces of bacteria or fungus can destroy the process. Use a 45-degree angle and make a cut as close as possible to the main stem without affecting the stem itself. As soon as you cut the plant, place it in a container of water immediately. What you are essentially doing is preventing the plant from being exposed to the air.

GREENHOUSE GARDENING

Now you can choose from different methods to clone your plant.

Method 1

In this method, you will use rockwool. More specifically, you should find rockwool cubes, as they are perfect for this technique. Place the rockwool cubes in water and allow them to soak for several hours.

Next, you should use a rooting hormone on the branch. If you have a powdery form of rooting hormone, then you can dip the plant in water and press the top of the root on the hormone. You only need to make sure that the hormone touches the bottom part of your branch (that part that is cut off from the main plant).

Then simply place the branch into the rockwool. Ensure that the bottom end of your branch is in contact with the rockwool.

Once that is done, you only have to take care of the branch until it grows. You can use a simple spray to apply a little moisture to the growing area.

Additionally, make sure you place the entire setup under sunlight. Again, place it under moderate sunlight. You could also get yourself some artificial lights to help you with the process, but make sure you get one for cloning.

Method 2

In this method, you can make use of a pot with soil. If you still have the pot that housed the plant you took the branch from, then that would be ideal for this scenario. However, you can use any pot. The only thing that you have to make sure of is that the soil is saturated.

Once again, apply the rooting hormones at the base of your branch and then place it into the soil.

It is as easy as that!

Method 3

For this technique, you can make use of a container filled with water. Ensure the water is at room temperature before starting out.

Your next step is to cover the opening or mouth of the container. You can do this by using a plastic wrap or aluminum foil.

Once you have covered the container, use a sharp object to create a hole in the top. All you have to do now is put the branch through the opening.

To make sure this technique works properly, get a

container with enough depth to make sure that the branch is at least 5 cm deep into the water.

And that is all there is to it!

CHAPTER 7

HOW TO GROW WITHOUT SOIL

Whenever someone mentions the word garden, you might imagine an arrangement of vegetables, flowers, or crops. You might also imagine a gardener with his or her tools. There could be a greenhouse. And of course, plenty of soil!

Because, without soil, there can never be plants right?

Right?

Well, not exactly.

Now let us try another scenario. You are now stepping into a greenhouse. You see pipes everywhere. And from these pipes, you can see plants sprouting, In fact, you notice different kinds of plants everywhere in the greenhouse.

How is this possible?

Where is the soil? Is this sorcery?!

Not really. Just science, and a lot of innovation.

Scientists discovered that while soil holds the nutrients essential for plant growth, the soil itself is not necessary for the plant itself.

So in the absence of soil, what else can you make use of?

The answer might surprise you (actually, it might not). You use water. You see, there is a technique called hydroponics, where you grow plants in water that contains all the essential nutrients for the plants.

The factors that affect successful plant growth are the various mineral nutrients present in the soil. These nutrients include potassium, nitrogen, and other substances. What if you could transfer all of these nutrients from soil into water? That way, you do not need to have different water for different plants, unlike soil.

One of the main reasons for adopting hydroponics is the fact that you may not always find the right kind of soil everywhere. You might have to make do with the soil you have close to you. This means that you have to invest in getting the right kind of fertilizer and other materials to enrich the soil with nutrients, balance its pH levels, make it moist, and work with it until you are ready to introduce it to the plants.

Hydroponics systems have also been known to increase the growth of plants tremendously. This might become useful for those gardeners who might face unpredictable weather patterns in their country and have to make sure that their crops are planted at the right time.

For hydroponics to be successful, you will require the right equipment. However, that does not mean you cannot try to grow plants in water at home. Do note that without the right technology, you might have to wait a while to see the results.

Here is how you can get started.

Step 1

You need to find yourself either a houseplant or a vegetable plant of your choice.

Step 2

When you have the plant, remove the soil from the roots.

Step 3

Fill a container with water and wait for it to settle down to room temperature.

Step 4

Once the water reaches room temperature, simply cover the container with either plastic wrap or foil. You can use other materials for this purpose, but ideally, the aforementioned options should work well.

Step 5

Punch in a hole through the material and place the plant into the hole. You should have the bottom of the plant submerged in at least 6 cm of water.

Step 6

Wait for a week. Remove the water, refill the container,

and add in plant food. Rewrap the opening of the container as we had discussed in Step 4.

Repeat this process every week.

There you have it! Your very own homemade hydroponic system.

CHAPTER 8

GROUND VERSUS CONTAINER

While hydroponics sounds like a nice idea, some people are more used to the traditional forms of gardening. They like to get their hands dirty and watch the progress of the plants that they grow. I can definitely relate to the satisfaction of that process!

However, when planting in soil, you often come up with the question: should I plant in the ground, or should I use containers like raised beds or pots?

So before we get into the details, let us try to understand one essential difference. After all, it cannot be just about having a ground to work on versus working inside a small container. When you are planting in the ground, you are making use of the topsoil. This is essentially dirt.

When you make use of a container, you are not using dirt. In fact, the soil used in containers is technically artificial soil.

The distinction can differ based on the container and the materials you use, but essentially, this is a distinction that you need to be aware of.

So which one is better?

If you have a large plot that is exposed to the sun, has a rich soil, and a proper drainage system for the soil, then you should choose the ground to plant. This is because you not only spend less on getting raised beds and adding soil and other materials into them, you also already have all the groundwork done for you. One thing to note here is that if you have soil like clay or sand that does not provide many nutrients, then you are better off trying to use a container. You can, of course, make sure that the clay and sandy soil is ready for planting, but that takes some extra steps. If you are not planning to invest the time in soil preparation (and maintaining that soil), then you might as well choose to plant inside a container.

When you are working on a raised bed, do note that you still have a considerable amount of work to perform in the beginning. However, once you have gotten the basic preparations ready, then your work for each season is less. What you are trying to do with a raised bed is create an artificial environment to make sure that your plants grow properly. The best thing about raised beds is that you can choose the height of the beds based on the plants that you want to grow. This makes it easier for you to remove weeds. If you have a short raised bed, you might extract weeds without much trouble. This might not be possible when working with ground. You might have to exert a lot of effort to remove weeds from the ground.

Finally, you can grow your plants in pots. There are a surprising number of people who prefer these small containers for their planting purposes. One of the main reasons is that pots occupy little space. This way, you can use them to grow your favorite plants and use them as decoration. If you are decorating, I would not suggest bringing them inside the home. With the dangers of pests and fungi, you might have a little health hazard within your home. Pots allow you to grow the exact number of plants that you want to (owing to their small size). Additionally, pots are easier to move around. So if you need more sunlight, you can easily transfer the pot to another location. Moreover, you can maintain pots easier than the ground or raised beds. The major drawback about pots is that the plants can dry out faster. This means that you need to make constant checks into the water level of the pot. Furthermore, once the soil has been used for a plant, you may not be able to use it again. Pot soils tend to lose their nutrients after they have grown a particular crop. But this might not be a hassle for those who are not planning to spend considerable time on gardening but would still like to enjoy the process. I also recommend pot planting to newcomers. This will help them get a feel for the process. Plus, it is much less expensive than the other two methods.

CHAPTER 9

POLLINATION

Pollination sounds like something the bees do. And actually, that is correct.

But before we get into bees, let us see what pollination itself means.

In short, it is a process of fertilization. It involves transferring pollen from the anther of the flower (considered the male) to the stigma (considered the female) of the plant. This allows for the plant to reproduce and generate seeds.

Now here comes the tricky part. How do flowers get the pollen from one part to the other? They depend on external forces named vectors. These vectors come in different forms. You have the wind, which blows the pollen to the necessary parts. You also have water performing the same act. But apart from the elements, you have creatures such as, you might have guessed it, bees. There are also butterflies, bats, and other birds that help in the process.

So as you can see, pollination is a complex process.

You can pollinate plants in your greenhouse, as well. The process can take a few tries to master, but once you get it, it is fairly easy. So how do you pollinate?

Let us examine a few techniques.

Pollinating Manually

This method is cost-effective. You only require your hands and the plants that you would like to pollinate. Simply tap or shake the plant or flower that you would like to pollinate. This process disperses the pollen from the male anther to the female parts. For certain plants, you might have to make the transfer happen. For example, plants such as squash have separate flowers for the male and the female. This is why you have to take the male pollen and bring it to the female flower. For other plants such as tomatoes, the setup is much more unique. Remember how we saw that the tomato is actually a fruit? That is the reason why its male and female parts are within the same flower (meaning: you don't have to worry about pollination, as tomatoes make the transfer themselves).

Pollinating By Using Devices

You can also purchase special battery-operated tools to assist you with the process of pollination. These tools produce a steady vibration that you simply have to place at the base of the flower. This encourages the flower to disperse the pollen into the air. You do not have to worry about any damage caused by these tools. They are specifically designed for the purpose of pollination.

Pollination by Bees

Of course, no one can do it like the bees! You could also get a box of bees (or a hive of bees) and introduce them into your greenhouse. This is the best way to pollinate your pants because you are leaving the work to the experts! However, you might need to have the right equipment and clothing to work with this method. You can get your hands on special bees raised for greenhouse pollination, along with a nectar that acts as their food source. Regardless, always consult with an expert on what is the best way to allow the bees into your garden and what precautions you must take (like trying to avoid leaving openings in your greenhouse, else the bees escape!).

GREENHOUSE GARDENING

CHAPTER 10

GROWING FRUITS, HERBS AND VEGETABLES

Before we begin looking at how to grow plants in your garden, here is an important note: I will be using the term annuals and perennials from here on out, so it might be the right time to introduce you to these terms.

Annuals are plants and crops that have a life cycle lasting for a year. They grow and produce seeds before dying in one season. This is why you have to replace annuals after each season.

Perennials are plants that produce yields from one year to the next. They usually live for more than two years. You do not have to replace perennials each year.

However, if you would like to introduce fresh perennials, then you may remove the previous plant.

Now that you are aware of the differences, it is time to add a little sweetness to your garden. What do I mean? We are going to begin with fruits.

Before we get started, here are a few notes.

- Growing fruits in your garden takes time. They also require more care than other plants and crops that you are planning to introduce to your garden. You do have species of fruits like certain berries and grapes that produce their sweet and juicy yield within a few months. The majority of fruits however, require patience and attention.

- When gardeners mention the word 'fruit', they usually group together three types of plants; fruits, nuts, and berries. The main reason for this is because there are not a lot of differences in the way that each plant is grown. Hence, for the sake of making explanations easier, I will use the term fruit broadly to denote fruits, nuts, and berries.

Let us dive into an interesting fact, as well. You see, a fruit is any structure that has the capability to bear seeds. This is why what you might typically consider as a vegetable is actually a fruit. We had already seen that the tomato is an example of a fruit. But did you know that the even cucumbers and peppers are fruits as well?

Just a little fruit for thought in case you were planning to grow cucumbers as vegetables.

Fruits

When you decide to grow a fruit, the most important factor that you should consider is choosing the right type of fruit for your garden. This choice is all it takes to ensure that you can grow the fruit well. I can understand the feeling of growing a specific type of fruit (which would typically be your favorite). However, before you decide that, try and perform a little research ahead of time.

Here is something you should know about fruit (thought I have a feeling some of you may already know this). Fruits do not appear immediately in a plant's life cycle. The flowers begin to boom first (which is a beautiful sight). Then, the petals of the flower begin to strip away. During this process, you will notice the fruit slowly swelling.

Some kinds of fruits are not suitable for growing in a garden. For example, dates are tough to grow and take more attention and work than other types of fruits. But that does not mean you are deprived of choice. Let me introduce you to the usual suspects.

You can successfully grow the following fruits in your garden:

Avocado, plum, cherry, apricot, apple, pear, banana, plum, kumquat, loquat, guava, pineapple, fig, nectarine, crabapple, pomegranate, persimmon, strawberry, blackberry, blueberry, raspberry, kiwi, any citrus fruits, gooseberry, and grapes.

See? You do have a lot of options.

Some of the fruits mentioned above are annuals, while others are perennials. This means that each fruit requires different times before they show their yield. You might consider this factor as well so that you can choose if you want a plant that has a faster yield or you are comfortable waiting.

Next, each fruit grows well in a particular climate. Pick your fruit based on that factor so that you are ready to provide the essential nutrients and growing conditions for the fruit. For example, if it is winter in your region and you would like to grow avocados, then you must know that avocados do not grow well in cold seasons. This means that you might have to pick another flower before you enter the right season for avocados.

If you want to know what fruits are ideal for your particular climate, then you can take inspiration from the local stores and farms. What fruits are not in demand? What are the farmers producing in abundance? Which fruit can you easily find in the local supermarket?

Size

You must also think about the size of the fruit that you are planning to grow. Think of how each fruit you grow fits into your greenhouse. If you are growing melons, then they might require more space then blueberries. Will you be able to provide this space? If you can, then how many melons can you grow at one time? Is that better than growing grapes, where you can get a higher yield? Plus, remember that gardening is also about aesthetics. You can make different arrangements of your fruits to create a beautiful display when the fruits appear. If you have the space to arrange different fruits, then you should think of how to make that arrangement. Here are a few tips that you can follow:

You can use kiwi fruits to act as boundaries. Do note that the kiwi is a clambering fruit, so you might either require a surface to support it or you might need to plant stakes into the ground or container for growing the plant. Either way, kiwis make beautiful boundaries.

You can plant berries around your property, or against a particular wall.

If you have an archway or a pergola, then you could use kiwi or grapevine for that. Just watch them cover it beautifully!

You can plant a fruit tree near the entrance to your garden or greenhouse.

Citrus trees or berry bushes can adorn the corners of your garden, drawing the eye towards them.

As the focal point of your garden, you can plant either berry bushes or fruit trees. Both add diversity and color to your garden. Other alternatives to this can be pear or plum trees.

If you are growing strawberries, think about the fact that you can grow them in hanging containers. Wonder where you could place that?

If you want to add ground cover in your garden, then you can pick any berry bush.

These are just some of the ways in which you can use fruits to bring life into your garden. How would you decorate your garden?

Pollination

Decide on how you would like to arrange your fruits to allow for proper pollination. You might have to ask the salesperson or supplier about the pollination process of the fruits you are buying. Sometimes, you might need to plant many plants of the same variety. In other cases, you have to use different varieties of the same species. Make sure you are well informed before raising these fruits.

Buy Plants, Not Seeds

If you are planning to use seeds to grow your fruit-bearing plants, then I recommend against it. Unless you do not mind waiting. For a long time!

Instead, choose to get the plant itself and start from there. Even when you are purchasing plants, make sure to keep in mind the below tips.

Buy high-quality plants

Do not compromise on quality, because this might affect the yield. If you want to enjoy a delicious and healthy yield, go for plants that have a high grade. Seek the advice of your local supplier in this matter.

Certified and Tested

Always look for proof that the plant you are about to purchase is certified for quality and tested against viruses. You do not need to get a plant in your garden only to realize it has a disease.

GREENHOUSE GARDENING

Inspect

Make your own inspection into the plant. Remember how you can find out if a plant has pest or diseases? Make sure you take the time to provide a detailed examination of the plant. My tip would first be to ask the supplier about the quality. Get an assurance and then perform your own check. This might also clue you into the honesty of the supplier (in case you want to decide on whether you want to return to the same store).

Planting the Fruit

Once you have decided on what fruits you would like to use for your garden, checked the sizes, and purchased the plant, you can now focus on the process of planting itself.

You might have already guessed this, but your first step should be to prepare the soil for the fruits. You can perform a soil test with a special kit to determine the quality of the soil. This might require a little investment from your side, but I highly recommend getting the kit. This is because once you are sure of the quality of your soil, you can be confident about the growth of your plants. Otherwise, you might spend more in the future trying to solve one problem after another. Once you have completed the soil test, you can send across the sample to a lab for results. If you cannot perform the soil test, then reach out to a local farmer or expert to tell you about the soil. If you are using containers, however, you can get your own soil for the fruit.

Next, you need to know what soil conditions are required for the fruit you want to grow. This means balancing the pH value of the soil. Some fruits might require a slightly acidic soil, while others may prefer content that is more alkaline.

You can also make use of organic fertilizers to prepare your soil. Look for experts who can guide you in that area.

Depth of Soil

This goes without saying, but if you are using a container, then make sure that the depth of the soil is sufficient for the roots of the fruits you are planning to grow. Ensure you arrange for the right container for each fruit-bearer. Trees might need a lot more depth than bushes, so you are ideally looking for a tall raised bed or a large pot.

Select the Time

For fruit-bearing plants, there is one trick that you can use: ensure that you have grown the plant as much as possible before it has to face the climate that causes it stress. This means planting well ahead. For cool-season fruits, a good tactic is to plant them during spring so that they can enjoy a wonderful summer before facing off against the biting winds of the winter.

For warm-season crops, your best bet is during fall or early winter. That way, they can mature enough before the sun becomes the fruit plants' enemy.

Taking Care

Once you have planted your fruits, it is then time to make sure that you take care of them properly. This means that you have to check their water, make sure that the fertilizer has been added, and perform other important actions.

Let us examine each step in detail.

Watering

While you are watering your plants, it is important to remember that adding too much water can drown the plant or even encourage the spread of diseases. In some scenarios, you might have added the right amount of water, but poor drainage does not deplete the used water in time, causing it to accumulate in the soil.

For fruit plants that have shallow roots, you might have to provide more water than is usually necessary. If there is rainfall, then your plants might get more water. However, you should still keep an eye on how much water your plant receives, because with little rain, you might have to pitch in.

I have talked about drip irrigation before, which I feel is perfect for growing your fruits. Here are two reasons why:

1. You can manage the supply of water to the fruits.
2. You can ensure that the fruits receive all the water that you supply to them.

Fertilizing

The main thing to note here is that if you have worked on your soil prior to planting your fruits, then you do not have to worry too much about maintaining the soil. I recommend adding a little fertilizer. However, do make sure that the fertilizer has a balanced pH. This means that it is neither too acidic nor too alkaline.

Mulch

For fruit-bearers, you do not have to worry about mulching too much. This is because fruit bearing plants cast enough shadow to keep weeds at bay.

Support

Sometimes, fruit plants may not have the strength to grow vertically, especially during the initial stages of their life cycle. When this happens, they often tend to lean in one direction. This causes them to fall on other plants, hindering the proper growth of both plants. In order to ensure that your fruit plant is maintaining a good distance from another fruit plant so that it can take in as much wind and sunlight as possible, you might have to add in support structures. You can drive stakes into the ground and allow the plants to grow with them. In some cases, you may remove the stakes later during the year once the plant can support itself. Stakes are usually made from wood, however, if you are using branches or sticks, make sure that they are thick. If you cannot find materials with sufficient thickness, then simply tie two branches or sticks together.

For other trees, you might have to place horizontal support lines. To form these lines, you drive two stakes into the ground such that the tree lies between the stakes. You then tie one end of a wire to one stake and the other end to the second stake. This way, you have a horizontal support line where the tree's branches can lie on these supports. Ideally, you need to set them at a height where the branches can lean on your support system. The wires can be of any material, provided that they are strong enough to hold the branches.

Pruning

For fruit-bearing plants, get your pruning tools ready; they might require you to attend to them regularly.

Here are two tips to keep in mind when pruning:

- Always make sure that the tools are cleaned properly. Dirty tools might spread diseases to the plants.

- Sharpness is important. Sharp tools cut through the plants in a clean manner. Blunt tools cause damage.

If at any time you feel that the work takes too much of your time, then stop planting more fruit-bearers. The entire process should be fun. While there are times when you might have to put in effort to make certain your plants are growing well, it should not feel like it is adding a lot of stress and difficulty to your life.

One way to approach this problem is to work on a small number of fruit-bearers. From there, you can decide if you would like to add more or add less to the entire arrangement. This helps you avoid a situation where you feel overwhelmed with all the work you are putting in (unless you don't mind, in which case, more is good!).

Herbs

If you look at the official definition for an herb, then it might mention that an herb is any plant that has leaves, flowers, or seeds used for a variety of purposes including flavouring, medicine, perfume or as ornamentals. However, what plants are herbs and which are not is sometimes too confusing to wrap your head around. Regardless, let us look at how we can grow these unique plants and add some spice to your garden!

Planting Herbs

One of the things you might notice about herbs is that there are no rules to follow with these plants. They can adapt to different conditions! Makes your job easier, doesn't it?

However, you do need to focus on the type of herb you are growing. Is it an annual herb or a perennial one? Does it require time to grow or can it grow quickly?

Timing

The thing about most herbs is that they cannot tolerate the cold. So ideally, you need to plant them just after the worst of the cold-temperatures have left the region. This way, you can let them utilize all the benefits of summer (sunlight and warm air in particular) before you get them ready for the winter.

Do not plant them in the heat of summer. They are not mature enough to handle the heat, which might cause them stress. If you would like to make use of herbs during winter time, then you could consider growing them in containers like pots and keeping them inside the greenhouse.

You could also use the below tips when planting herbs:

- Herbs require the same growing conditions as vegetables. So no need to focus on just one type of plant when you can grow multiple plants at the same time. This way, you can even manage to get your vegetables and herbs at the same time if everything goes well! Perfect for some delicious comfort food!

- Combining them with flowers is also another good idea. You can use the flowers when they are in bloom and at the same time, get your herbs as well. Additionally, you could even use the herbs in your flower arrangement. That sort of arrangement helps you create a beautiful display.

- Alternatively, you can create an herb garden. This is not just beautiful, but also helps you focus on your herbs entirely. For many people, they prefer to use their gardens just for herbs. This allows them to buy their vegetables but use the herbs from their own garden.

GREENHOUSE GARDENING

Planting Your Herbs

Unlike fruits, you might need to take special care when planting your herbs. Here are some tips for you to follow:

- Get your trowel ready. Find a nice spot that is covered by sufficient sunlight. Ideally, make sure you have well-drained soil. Once you find the spot, dig a hole into it. The size of the hole should be slightly bigger than the pot carrying the herb. Add compost and organic fertilizer. Seek out the help of local professionals to let you know which one you should use for the purpose.

- Now remove the plant from the pot. Remember never to pull the plant by its leaves. You have to get the plant intact, not with its leaves missing. If that happens, you don't have a plant anymore. You just have a stem!

- Now examine the stem of the plant. Look for a soil line. This is a line that shows where the soil ends and where you can see the stem clearly. You need to make sure that you plant the herb in the same depth as it had while it was in the pot (using the soil line for reference.)

If you choose to plant the herb in a container, then

make sure you follow the below steps:

- Choose a pot that has a big size. You might need it for the roots of the plant.

- Make sure the pot has a drainage hole at the bottom. If it does not have one, then you can create one for it. Be careful while doing so, because any work on the pot might shatter it.

- Finally, fill up the pot with potting soil mix. Make sure that the mix is damp.

- Remove the seedling from the herb you have with you and place it into the pot.

- Start watering it!

Caring for Your Herb

There is not much to do while taking care of herbs. You just have to make sure that you provide them with sufficient sunlight. They need a moderately fertile soil, so you should be good to go in that regard (provided you have utilized a good-quality organic matter). Drainage is important, because you need to make sure that they have enough water to survive but not too much to affect their growth.

Make sure that you do not utilize too much fertilizer. Use fertilizer sparingly. You could ask the supplier for assistance in this matter, as they know how to take care of the herb that you have bought from them.

Vegetables

Now we get to the good part - vegetables! There are so many to choose from. To get your vegetables in order, you must begin with the planning phase.

Location

Find a place in your garden where you would like to start. Make sure that you know what vegetable or vegetables you intend to plant. With a smaller space, you always have room to expand based on future decisions. For example, you might choose to add a different vegetable next to the one you are growing right now.

Take a piece of paper and draw out your vegetable layout. Do not use up all the space you have in your garden. Make sure you are giving enough space to add more vegetables when you see fit.

A lot of people underestimate the value of having a visual depiction of the entire plan. What you are essentially doing is making sure that you do not give away too much space to one vegetable.

When you are working with vegetables, do not leave

empty spaces. When you are done with one crop, then utilize that space to grow the next vegetable ideal for the coming season. For example, if you had just harvested a summer vegetable, then you should use the space available for a winter vegetable. However, this method is a little tricky, so expect some disappointments before you master the technique.

More Sunlight

When you are growing vegetables, then you need to make sure that you are working with the sun. There should not be obstacles nearby that block out sunlight. The sun not only helps the plant directly but also warms up the soil, keeping both plant and soil healthy. However, there are vegetables that require less sun. In such cases, you simply have to use a covering material such as a mesh or blind (as we had discussed before).

Planting Methods

You might be using the ground to plant your vegetables, or you might make use of a raised bed. You should approach both these surfaces differently when you are working with vegetables.

Natural Ground

When you are working on natural ground, make sure that the roots of the vegetables have sufficient space to grow. You might encounter sod, which is essentially grass and the soil that it holds. You can remove this layer effectively by using a spade.

If you encounter weeds as well, then make sure you have the right tools to get rid of them. You can always make use of a weeder to rip out weeds that are stubborn.

Raised Beds

With raised beds, you avoid all the work you put into the ground. You already have good drainage inside a raised bed and if you encounter weeds, you can remove them easily. Similar to using natural ground, make sure that you provide enough depth for the roots of the vegetables, depending on the vegetable of course. Use high-quality soil to fill up the raised bed. This is necessary because you might encounter less problems as you work with your vegetables.

Soil Tactics

Whether you prefer to use a natural bed or a raised bed, you need to make sure that the soil is in good condition for the plant.

Here are a couple of tips for you to use:

- When you dig to make space for the roots, you can dig a depth between 8 to 12 inches. This is sufficient for most vegetables. However, you should check again before planting the vegetable to ensure that you are making the right measurements.

- Make sure you add in as much organic fertilizer or matter as possible. You need to make the soil appropriate for the crop, or the vegetable might not even survive a couple of months!

Using Seeds

Gardeners often prefer to get their vegetables as seeds. When you are acquiring your vegetables, think of the time you want to spend on growing the plants, when you would like to harvest the vegetables, how much you are willing to spend, and how much effort you are willing to put into growing your vegetable. Seeds allow you to grow high-quality vegetables, since you will be providing the right growing conditions from the beginning of their life. However, they require more attention and time. Alternatively, you could get starter plants, which require less time to work on. The only drawback is that you have to be content with the quality they come in. You could make sure that you only purchase high-quality plants to ensure that you have a good crop growing in your garden.

GREENHOUSE GARDENING

Sowing Your Vegetables

If you have bought seeds, then you should make sure to sow them. Typically, you will have the instructions to sow on the packet itself. But, we will make sure to follow a few steps before we can begin sowing the seeds.

This process can be done indoors. All you have to do is make sure you have a good spot where there are fewer people. This means areas where there is less foot traffic. This way, nothing will disturb your lovely plants.

Once you have found your spot, follow the below steps:

- Make sure you are providing light to the area you are going to use for sowing. You could provide natural light or set up artificial light sources.

- Get a pot or a flat container. Add a seed-starting mix into the pot or container. Make sure that the mix is damp. Add water if necessary.

- Use your hands or any material to level the surface of the mix.

- Now, you just have to follow the instructions

on the seed packet and place the seeds into the seed-mix accordingly.

- Once you have placed the seeds, cover the entire container or pot with a plastic wrap. Pierce some holes into it and make sure that you do not tighten the wrap too much. It only needs to be secure enough to not fall off.

- Keep checking the container. Open the plastic wrap to make sure that the seeds breathe.

- Once they grow into seedlings, you are ready to shift them into a raised or natural bed in your garden.

Fertilizing Your Vegetable Garden

If you have been working on your garden for a while and it already has sufficient compost and fertilizers, then it is not required for you to add more. However, I still recommend that you add them just so you do not deprive your vegetables of essential nutrients.

When you are working with fertilizers, you typically get instructions on how to use them. Follow those instructions so that you do not use an excessive amount of those fertilizers.

Now all you need to do is take care of your vegetable patch and you will soon be the proud owner of your own collection of vegetables.

CHAPTER 11

GROWING FLOWERS AND PLANTS

Get ready to add a splash of color to your garden! And of course, we will be working with other plants. Like with fruits and vegetables, you have the choice between annual and perennial flowers.

While most people would recommend picking any one of the two varieties, I think you should start with the annuals. As these flowers use one season (typically about a year) to mature, you might start seeing the results of your work sooner.

Discover Flowers

So what kinds of flowers should you be looking for?

Well, it depends on the climate. You probably know where I am headed next. Yes, warm-season flowers and cold-season flowers.

Let us look at both these flowers below.

Warm Season Annuals

These flowers make use of the summer to thrive! They can tolerate long periods without water. Expert plant breeders would make use of this feature and work on these plants, often changing their look and color. These flowers are highly intolerant of the cold, so taking extra care of them during winter is important.

Cool Season Annuals

These flowers are the opposite of warm season flowers. They can withstand cold winters, but are incapable of surviving well during the summer. Breeders have combined these flowers with other flowers, often improving their resistance to the sun.

So what can you do with annuals? A lot! There is no limit to the amount of creativity you can add into the combinations of flowers.

What are some of the factors that you should consider when growing flowers? This depends on what you are trying to achieve with your flower bed. Are you planning to grow something for yourself? Would you like to create a work of art? Perhaps you are hoping to invite the birds and butterflies to join your garden. Everyone has a specific objective that they would like to achieve. Make sure you know what you would like to have happen within your flower bed.

Flower Garden Tips

Once you have your goals set in place, it is time to let your creativity flow.

Choosing Your Color Palette

The first thing that you should focus on is trying to create a palette. There are a few criteria you can consider when you are choosing your palette.

A color scheme is the best way to get started with flowers. When you have a scheme, you give yourself a group of colors to work with. This allows you to design your garden based on these colors, creating a wonderful uniformity. You see, it does sound nice in theory to add as much color as possible. But in practice, it only tends to cause exhaustion to the eyes. Plus, they do not look appealing.

To create a color palette, you simply have to use a wheel. Not literally, no. I mean a color wheel like the one below.

Using the wheel, you can create many different types of color palettes.

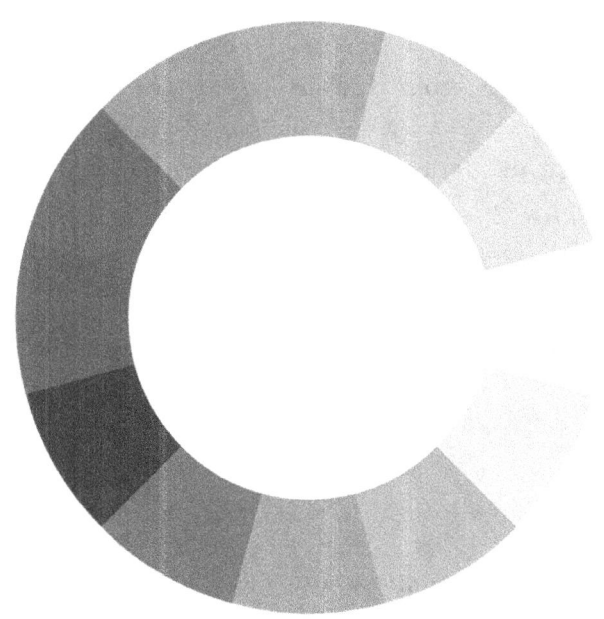

Option 1: Complimentary

For this option, you simply choose the color that lies in opposition from the color you start with. For example, let us assume that you chose sky blue as your first choice. To compliment this color, you should look for flowers that are orange (it lies on the opposite side)! However, once you choose your colors, you can further enhance the appearance by choosing different shades of the same color. For the orange, you could use a combination of darker and lighter oranges. For the blue, you could make use of sky blue and azure. Adding a slight variety in shades can help you create a breathtaking display that will make anyone stop in their tracks to stare at your handiwork. You might feel like Picasso, minus the paintbrush and with the addition of flower seeds.

Option 2: Analogous

With this option, you choose colors that lie next to each other. Using the color wheel above, you could go with blue and green. You could also try out red and magenta. These colors add a little boldness to your garden, but they create a wonderful effect in the end.

Option 3: Monochromatic

In this option, you can decide to stick to one shade. That might sound boring, but the results are far from it. You see, monochromatic shades belong to the same hues. Let us assume that you choose the color yellow, then plant flowers belonging to different shades of yellow. This creates a pleasing and comfortable visual to the eye. As there is just one color to focus on with different shades, the result can add a pleasing and calming effect to your design.

Option 4: Warmth

For this color scheme, you use all or some of the warm colors of the palette. This means that you can combine red, orange, and yellow for example. While working with these colors, you can also add in different shades to add a spectacular bright and sunny effect!

Option 5: Cool

You might have guessed it. In the color palette, you add in all the cool colors of the wheel. Throw in the blue. Add the green. Make use of the fuchsia. The result? You experience a calm and peaceful sight.

Working with the Shape of Your Flowers

Flowers present you with different shapes. You have daisies, spires, globes, plumes, and many others. You can combine different shapes to produce interesting effects.

With shapes, there is no right combination, because each individual may have different ideas when looking at the shapes of plants. Which is why it is up to you to experiment with combining different shapes and seeing what effects they produce. Variety is the spice, as they say!

Working with Layers

You can also take advantage of the different heights of plants to create a layer effect. While you are designing your layers, you can make use of a color palette from the options above. Let us assume that you have decided to work with warm colors. You could ideally have tall reds, followed by oranges, and using yellows for the final layer. Layers are perfect when you only have one small area to work with or are using flowers against the sides of walls.

Planting Your Flowers

Now that you've let out your inner artist, it's time to establish some groundwork. And by that, I mean planting the flowers you have chosen.

Some plants require a lot more sunlight than the others. Some plants actually thrive while staying in the shade for the majority of the day with exposure to sunlight just a few times a day. If you have chosen a particular color palette, then you can make use of shades or makeshift roofs for certain flowers that do not require too much sunlight.

The next thing you should work on is the soil. Most flowers grow best in garden soil that is loose and filled with lots of fertilizer or organic material.

Now is the time to plant your flowers. Make sure you have an arrangement ready for your flower beds. If you have not prepared an arrangement plan, then take a short while to figure out how to arrange your flowers.

Finally, water the flowers. You should ideally ensure that there is at least 1 to 2 inches of moisture in the soil. How do you know how much moisture is there in the soil? Well, remember our finger test? It is as simple as that!

As the flowers start growing, you can snip off some stems and use the flowers in a bouquet or an arrangement in your home. Once you have done so, snip off any protrusions so that the flower can divert energy to places that require it.

CHAPTER 12

GREENHOUSE BUSINESS

Working on your greenhouse eventually leads you to an important conclusion. You are actually growing plants, flowers, and crops. Aren't these in demand?

Can you sell what you produce?

Can you make a business out of your idea?

After all, you are not going to eat all the eggplants you grow. You might as well make use of the excess food.

Well, you definitely can make a business out of your greenhouse! When you have decided to grow your business, there are a few things that you have to consider.

Let us look at each.

Choose What You Want to Sell

If you are a beginner, you might still be trying to figure out how to work with plants. What you should figure out is what you are good at growing. Do you think that you can grow fruits really well? Can you harvest fresh vegetables? Are your flower growing skills excellent?

When you decide where you want to focus your attention, you can determine what you can sell.

Once you have figured out your area of expertise, try to research different techniques and ideas. Look at your local stores to find out what is popular. Let us assume that you are comfortable working with vegetables. Your next move should be to head over to the local grocer and find out what vegetables are in season. You could also take advantage of media and news outlets to give you inspiration. For example, if avocados are growing in popularity, then maybe you can exploit that situation to create a business revolving around that opportunity.

It Is Not All About Numbers

A lot of people think that you can only sell by growing hundreds of plants. While that could be true if you were a farmer, there is no reason why you cannot turn your garden into a small hobby business.

The idea is to make decide how much you would like to sell in the market. This will allow you to grow plants for yourself and for your home business.

Selling Your Plants

There are numerous ways to sell what you have grown. Here are some of the ways that I think might help you get started:

Farmer's Market

Many cities have a farmer's market. You could invest in a small stand for yourself and establish what you are going to sell in that market. I know it is rather tempting to sell vegetables one day and then show the world your skills in growing flowers the next. However, I would recommend sticking to one kind of plant. This will help people recognize you. You could, however, experiment with what people like the most in a market by offering different items.

Online Listings

There are numerous gardens that make a business through online or local listings. These listings are typically free, so you can go ahead and create a nice ad for yourself. When you begin to list your products, you also create an effective marketing process for yourself.

Yard Sales

There are no shortage of yard sales in the city, so go ahead and make the most out of them. For a yard sale, I would recommend bringing in the best of all your offerings. Get the best fruits, vegetables, and even add in some flowers. This variety will let people know about your products. But most importantly, it will let them decide what they would like to expect from you. Perhaps they are more interested in your vegetables. Your fruits could definitely be the highlight of the day. Or even your flowers might steal the show.

Marketing Your Garden

One of the things that you can do to help your garden is to effectively market it. Start off by establishing a marketing strategy. You need to take into account all of the available means for you to market your garden. These could be in the form of print materials or by using the bulletin board at your local supermarket. Whatever you choose, here are a few recommendations from my end.

Create Flyers

Flyers are visually striking (and they allow you to create a logo for yourself, which is an awesome feeling by itself). In the flyers, make sure that you list your products as well. Add in some style! Bring in the colors! Don't go overboard with the colors, though. A tip would be to add colors that give out a natural feel, like greens and yellows. Once you have your flyers ready, get the help of your friends and family to distribute them. You could even use the farmer's market and the yard sales as a way to distribute your flyers. Here is another tip: set up a small holder or stand on which you can display your flyers as well. Every time a customer makes a purchase, throw in your flyer for good measure!

Word-of-Mouth

The next thing you could try is to give away items to people who live near you. Offer them your first batch of produce for free and let them know that if they enjoyed your products, they could let others know about you, as well. If you create a good impression, you might just have a line of people waiting to get your stuff! For an effective word-of-mouth, make sure that you are giving away stuff to people who are close to you. These people could include your friends, family, and neighbors.

Create a Classifieds Ad

Typically, this should not cost you a fortune if all you are doing is placing a small ad. If you do not have a budget to add pictures in your ad, then make sure that your text is catchy and informative. Here is an example:

"Fruits! Vegetables! Flowers! Home grown products in your neighbourhood."

What you should aim to do is dispense with lengthy content and add a short catchy description. Most people do not have the time to sit through a long reading. So, you might as well throw in all the attractive and necessary info while you have their short attention span.

Make sure that you add in your contact details. Imagine grabbing their attention, but forgetting to tell them who to contact!

Open a Social Media Page

In today's world, social media is an effective way to spread the word about your products. Create a Facebook and Instagram page, along with any other social media platform that is popular in your area. Start creating frequent content about your garden. Add in beautiful pictures (daylight pictures using a high-definition camera or mobile phone with an excellent camera). Throw in the occasional video as well. Introduce yourself on camera so that people know the person behind the lovely creations. Occasionally introduce some interesting facts about the products that you are growing. For example, show them the apples you have been growing and then talk about what makes apples special. What about them can interest your audience? Or is there anything they would like to know about the particular species of apples growing in your garden? Here is an important point to note: regularly post on your social media page. Do not start working on it only to let it die down from lack of activity.

CONCLUSION

Don't feel like it all has to be perfect! When you start gardening, it is easy to think that you are going to get everything right. You want everything to be perfect. Every minute detail should be looked out for.

This is not necessary.

The most important factor for you to consider is that you should enjoy the process.

Let the mistakes happen. You end up learning more about the process that way. You gain more insights into the techniques you are using. You understand how a specific plant should be grown.

Gardening has been known to create a calming effect on people. That should be the case with you, too. There is no point stressing out over everything. Simply take your time with each step and should you encounter a mistake, shrug it off and find a solution. In fact, when you find a solution, you end up learning how to solve the problem, should it occur in the future.

Albert Einstein said, "Learning is an experience. Everything else is just information."

I say - time to experience gardening.

GREENHOUSE GARDENING

www.ingramcontent.com/pod-product-compliance
Lightning Source LLC
Chambersburg PA
CBHW071207070526
44584CB00019B/2945